Victor Hugo, Paul Meurice

The Letters of Victor Hugo: from Exile, and after the Fall of the Empire

Victor Hugo, Paul Meurice

The Letters of Victor Hugo: from Exile, and after the Fall of the Empire

ISBN/EAN: 9783743306530

Manufactured in Europe, USA, Canada, Australia, Japa

Cover: Foto ©ninafisch / pixelio.de

Manufactured and distributed by brebook publishing software (www.brebook.com)

Victor Hugo, Paul Meurice

The Letters of Victor Hugo: from Exile, and after the Fall of the Empire

THE LETTERS OF
VICTOR HUGO

THE LETTERS OF

VICTOR HUGO

FROM EXILE, AND AFTER THE
FALL OF THE EMPIRE

EDITED BY

PAUL MEURICE

BOSTON AND NEW YORK
HOUGHTON, MIFFLIN AND COMPANY
The Riverside Press, Cambridge
1898

Copyright, 1898,
By HOUGHTON, MIFFLIN & CO.

All rights reserved.

The Riverside Press, Cambridge, Mass., U. S. A.
Electrotyped and Printed by H. O. Houghton and Company.

NOTE.

In this translation of the second volume of the Letters of Victor Hugo some letters of minor interest have been omitted, and a few notes have been given in addition to those supplied by the French editor.

CONTENTS.

		PAGE
I.	LETTERS TO VARIOUS PERSONS. — JOURNEY ON THE RHINE	1
II.	THE COUP D'ETAT. — LETTERS FROM BRUSSELS	55
III.	LETTERS FROM EXILE	115
IV.	AFTER THE FALL OF THE EMPIRE	235

THE LETTERS OF VICTOR HUGO.

I. LETTERS TO VARIOUS PERSONS. — JOURNEY ON THE RHINE.
1836–1851.

I.

To MLLE. LOUISE BERTIN, *at Les Roches.*

MONT SAINT-MICHEL, 27*th June,* 1836.

I AM writing to you, mademoiselle, from Mont Saint-Michel, which is really the most beautiful spot in the world, — next to Bièvre, of course. Les Roches is lovely and charming; a great advantage it possesses over the forbidding mass of dungeons, towers, and rocks which bears the name of Mont Saint-Michel.

It would not be easy to write from a more awe-inspiring place to a more delightful one. At this moment I am hemmed in by the sea which surrounds the mount. It must be horrible in winter, with its hurricanes, tempests, and shipwrecks. It is grand, all the same.

What a strange place Mont Saint-Michel is! Around, as far as the eye can reach, infinite space, the blue horizon of the sea, the green horizon of the land, clouds, air, liberty, birds in full flight, ships with all sails set, and then all at once, on the top of an old wall above our heads, through a barred window, the pale face of a prisoner. I have never felt so strongly as here the cruel antithesis which man sometimes makes with nature.

You can have none of these sad thoughts. You are happy over there; happy with your excellent father, your kind relations; happy in the view of your beautiful valley from your window; happy in the prospect of your great success.

I shall be in Paris between the 10th and 15th of July, quite at your disposal, and ready for *Notre-Dame*,[1] a poor plaster statue of which I can see from the casement of my room, perched in a beautiful trefoil niche of the fifteenth century.

II.

To LOUIS DE MAYNARD, *at Martinique.*

24th *May*, 1837.

We are still expecting you. Your kind and charming letter told us you were soon returning; we were all looking forward to it, and you have not yet arrived!

We want you badly here; we want you for ourselves, because we love you, and for my part because your generous and loyal friendship was one of the real joys of my life; then we want you for your own sake, because here, I am sure, you would write us a fine book. We want you for the ideas which you would promote for art, which has so few followers like yourself; we want you because a noble, honest face like yours, erect

---

[1] *La Esmeralda*, for which Mlle. Bertin was composing the music.

amid so many drooping and sidelong glances, rests the eye and consoles the heart.

At any rate, I hope you are doing something over there. Make up for your absence by some fine work, your natural product. Instead of the great human stage which you had here, you have the grand spectacle of nature; instead of the strife of ideas, you have the placid harmony of things; if you have less of the world, you have more sunshine. As for me, I continue my task, waters much troubled, as you know, by the stones thrown into them; I work, I study, I have three plays in my head, — you shall see one some of these days, — and then occasionally I write poetry.

Our politics are still mean and petty, you remember; they have not improved since you left us. Small men working at a small idea, very little busy about nothing.

Altogether, there are times when I envy you, — you a poet exiled in a sunny land, an exile which Ovid would have loved, in that beautiful Martinique which you have described so admirably.

My fraternal love to you.

III.

To A Workingman and Poet.

Paris, 3d *October*, 1837.

Be proud of your title of workman. We are all workmen, God included, and in your case the brain works still more than the hands.

The generous class to which you belong has a great future in store for it, but it must give the fruit time to ripen. This class, so noble and so useful, should eschew what makes little and seek what makes great; it should try to discover reasons for love rather than pretexts for hatred; it should learn to respect women and children; it should read and study in its leisure moments; it should develop its intelligence, and it will achieve success. I have said in one of my works: *The day when the people becomes intelligent, it will rule.* In other words, civilization is the paramount thing. Sometimes it rules through one man, as with the popes; sometimes through more than one, as with the senates; sometimes through all, as will be the case with the people. Patience, therefore. Let us understand what exists, to be worthy of existence some day. Let the people work, for we all work. Let it love us, for we love it. Let it not disturb the young plant, barely sown, if it wishes to enjoy shade and fruit in the future.

I am sure that all these ideas are yours as well. Impress them on the people, of which your intelligence makes you one of the natural leaders. Instead of simply thanking you for your excellent verses, so flattering to me, I have indulged in this serious conversation. You will, I imagine, accept it as I offer it, as a token of sympathy and esteem.

IV.

To VICTOR PAVIE.

28th November, 1837.

You are quite right to continue to think a little of your friends in the Place Royale. You are loved here, — *loved,* do you understand? — and with all our hearts. You know, my dear Pavie, that friendship is a religion to me. And besides, who can be a better friend than you? My wife and I often say this to each other in the winter evenings, when we think of the many false faces which have betrayed us. A friend such as you are is a good and noble thing.

Here I am troubled by worries, legal business,[1] lawyers, and annoyances of every description. You must have seen something of this in the papers; but what they do not tell you is that my thoughts are very often with you amidst all the whirl.

David has given you my bust. I congratulate it; it will henceforth be present at your intimate conversation and family talks; I envy it.

Amid the tumult which my enemies raise around me, I have built up a little sanctuary into which I gaze unceasingly. In it are my wife and my children, the sweet and happy side of my existence.

Do come and see us this winter. Bring Theodore; bring your good father. I do not say, Bring your wife, for when I am speaking to you I naturally include her.

V.

To LAMARTINE.

14*th May*, 1838.

You have written a grand poem, my friend. *La chute d'un ange* is one of your most majestic creations. What will be the edifice, if these are only the bas-reliefs! Never has the breath of nature more deeply penetrated and more amply inspired a work of art, from the base to the summit, and in its minutest details.

I thank you for the happy hours which I have just spent closeted with your genius. I fancy that I have an ear for your voice. Consequently my admiration for

---

[1] Lawsuit with the *Comédie Française*.

you comes not only from my soul, but from my heart; for with a poet like you, to create is to charm, and with a listener like me, to admire is to love.

Yours *ex imo pectore.*

VI.

To M. VEDEL, *Manager of the Comédie Française.*

MONTMIRAIL, 20*th August*, 1838.

DEAR SIR, — According to the terms of the judgment given in the suit between me and the *Comédie Française*, and confirmed by decree, the *Comédie* was to play *Angelo* a certain number of times between the 20th of November, 1837, and the 20th of April, 1838, under a penalty of fifty francs damages for every day of delay. At the present date, August the 20th, the number of performances has not been completed, and the result is that at this moment the *Comédie Française* is indebted to me in the sum of eighteen thousand francs. However, I see no reason for altering the decision which led me to remit the sum of two thousand four hundred francs owing to me by the *Comédie* for delays in the representation of *Marion de Lorme*. I am even delighted to have this further opportunity of personally acknowledging the amiability and good taste of which you have given me more than one proof in our recent intercourse. I must add that I am glad to be able to convey my thanks also to those actors of the *Comédie Française* who have assisted me with so much zeal and talent. Be so good then, dear sir, as to inform the *Comédie* that I give it a free and full discharge of the sum of eighteen thousand francs which it now owes me. VICTOR HUGO.

VII.

To M. Etcheverry, *at the Ecoles newspaper office.*
27th February, 1839.

... I read your *Gazette des Ecoles* with great interest. In this paper, as in everything that comes from the rising generation, there is something noble and honest which expands the heart.

Courage, gentlemen, courage! you belong to the generation which owns the future. You will do great things. In politics you will finish the rough sketches; in literature you will carry on the work. For a long time past in all my writings I have striven to hasten the day when social questions will be substituted for political ones; when, between the party of reaction and that of revolution, there will arise the party of civilization. That day will be yours; that party will consist of you.

In spite of all that is said, the age in which we live is a grand one. At no other time have art and thought soared so high. On all sides there are great beginnings of everything. Congratulate yourselves, for you will have many a sacred task to accomplish. As for me, I view the innumerable questions which are rising in every quarter without anxiety, for I foresee the genius of the coming age, and I know that you will have plenty of solutions to offer.

VIII.

To MME. VICTOR HUGO.

Tuesday, 27th August, 1839.

I have finished my third act,[1] dearest. It is almost as long as the first, so that my play is already as long as an ordinary one.

I am feeling so unwell, and the loneliness of the house is so unbearable to me, that I am going away. I shall write my last act when I return. It will be no loss, for I am worn out with fatigue, and if I were to go on working now I believe I should fall ill. When I come back I shall be set up again, and I shall finish it in a week. So all is for the best.

I hope you have had a good and pleasant journey. I fancy I can see you comfortably settled in my kind friend Vacquerie's house. Take a good rest, my Adèle, enjoy yourself, and tell all my little darlings to have plenty of fun, and to be very happy. I am always thinking of you all, and I pray God to keep you happy.

I hope, also, that Charles and Toto are working hard, as they are bound to do, as befits those who have gained a prize.

Kiss my beloved Didine, my good little Dédé, my dear little Toto, and my dear old Charlie, and my fondest love to yourself. I love you.

Your own   VICTOR.

[1] Of the play *Les Jumeaux*, which was never finished.

IX.

To Jules Lacroix.[1]

14th April, 1840.

You are perfectly right, dear poet; make the translation homogeneous. In the French language there is a great gulf between prose and poetry; in English there is hardly any difference. It is a splendid privilege of the great literary languages — Greek, Latin, and French — that they possess a *prose*. English has not this privilege. There is no prose in English. The genius of the two languages is, therefore, completely different in this respect. What Shakespeare was able to do in English he would certainly not have done in French. So obey your excellent poetical instinct; do in French what Shakespeare would have done, what Corneille and Molière have done, write homogeneous pieces.

That is my advice. And, next, I am devotedly attached to you.

X.

To Mme. Victor Hugo, *at Saint-Prix.*

Paris, *31st July,* 1840.

I send you a very good piece of news, dearest, as quickly as possible. Charles[2] has gained the first prize for an essay in the open competition. M. Jauffret gave it out this morning before all his class in the college.

---

[1] Jules Lacroix, who translated several of Shakespeare's plays into French verse, had asked Victor Hugo if it would be better to translate Shakespeare entirely into Alexandrine verse, or to mix up prose and verse as in the English text.

[2] Charles Hugo, eldest son of the poet.

When he came to Charles's name the whole class burst forth; there were three rounds of applause. The dear boy is very happy. I have seen him twice to-day, as well as M. Poirson [1] and M. Jauffret. Are you not also delighted? Kiss our dear little girls for me. I love you fondly, my Adèle.

Here is the letter I received from M. Poirson:—

I wish to congratulate you to-day, dear sir, and to sympathize with your paternal joy and pride. There have been many more glorious and more intoxicating moments in your life, but can there have been a happier one? A. POIRSON.

XI.

To MME. VICTOR HUGO, *at Saint-Prix.*

PARIS, 29*th August, noon* [1840].

I am off in a few minutes, dear Adèle, and I am writing to you as I promised. I am in low spirits. I love you dearly, darling, and at this moment I wish you could know how tenderly I think of you all, my beloved ones.

I am going via Soissons, as I did last year. I notice that it is always easier to get places for the North than for the South.

Tell my Charles and my Toto that I shall be very pleased with them if they work hard.

I will write to you from my first stopping-place. My fondest love to you all, my Didine, my Dédé, my little prizemen, and my kindest regards to your dear father.

Love me, my Adèle, and think a little of me.

[1] Headmaster of the Collège Charlemagne.

XII.

To THE SAME.

NAMUR, 2d *September*, 1840.

I am at Namur, dearest, and I am sending you the first pages of my diary. In future I will send it you in this form, for in this way I shall be able to keep apart, as you wish, what concerns the journey and what concerns us. It will therefore be a diary [1] pure and simple, to which I will always add a letter to you. I am starting for Liège, and from there I go to Cologne.

I think of you all very tenderly, and of you, my Adèle. I hope you are all well at Saint-Prix, and that the fine air and lovely country are doing your dear father as much good as ever.

I beg my dear children and you to write me really nice long letters. I need them more than ever when I am traveling. Nature is charming, but family affection is still more so.

Do not let any one but members of the family read this diary of mine. I shall be delighted if it amuses and interests you and your father a little. If by chance there is any one not of the family at Saint-Prix, even an intimate friend, I beg you not to let him read the diary. I have already pointed out to you the danger of so doing. Good-by, dearest; my very best love to you all, my dear ones; I think only of you.

[1] This diary was intended to form, and eventually did form, the book called *Le Rhin*.

XIII.

To Mme. Victor Hugo.

St. Goar, 15*th September*, 1840.

I am continuing my journey up the Rhine slowly, as you see, dearest. Here is the continuation of my diary. I try to see everything, so as to have a complete and distinct idea of this beautiful country.

I cannot remember the date of Marie de Medici's death, nor that of Rubens' birth. Your father is sure to know them. Ask him to fill in the spaces I have left blank. If he were with me, which would be a delight to me, I should not leave any.

I have made a sketch of Andernach for my little Didine, but it is too large to go into a letter. It would have to be folded. I am keeping it in my album to give you in Paris, my darling Didine. I have left Andernach, and am now at St. Goar, a wonderful place, of which I will send you a drawing of some sort.

I travel slowly because I must do so, and yet I am sorry to do so, for I long to reach Mayence, where your letters are awaiting me, my dearest Adèle, my darling children; I hope they will bring me only what is sweet and good. I am always thinking tenderly of you; you are with me everywhere, in my expeditions and in my work.

Good-by, dearest; good-by, my Adèle. Think of me and love me. I will soon write again. Go on writing to Mayence. I will write to you all from Mayence, for I hope you will all have written to me. Fondest love to you, and also to your kind father. Kisses for you, dearest, for you, my Didine, for you, my Charles, to you both, my Toto and Dédé. You must all think of your father, who loves you so dearly.

XIV.
To THE SAME.

AIX-LA-CHAPELLE, 25*th September*, 1840.

I think, dearest, you must have already received the first twelve pages of my diary. I am now sending you the next installment, hoping greatly that it may interest you all a little. I am at Aix-la-Chapelle, and I leave for Cologne to-morrow. From there I intend to go up the Rhine as far as possible. In a few days I will send you the account of my journey from Liège to Aix-la-Chapelle. Tell Didine [1] to follow me on the map. I hope to get good news of you all at Mayence, for I want it badly. It seems an age since I left you all, and I feel quite sad when I recall my poor Toto's tearful face on old Bontemps' doorstep.

Work well, my dear children. My Charlie, remember you are now among the clever boys of the fifth form. You also, Toto, will soon begin your school life; you must do it with credit. Play well, too. Write me long letters, — all of you, mind, — my beloved ones, my dear little Dédé included. I hope her chicken, her pigeon, her kid, her cat, and her rabbit will not keep her from writing to her papa. I beg she will work well, and be very obedient to her sister, who is a sensible girl. I do not mean by this that Dédé is not a good child. I hope her dear kind mamma is pleased with her.

Tell your father, my Adèle, that I miss him every

---
[1] Léopoldine, Victor Hugo's eldest daughter.

moment in this charming journey, in which everything would interest him; I have no books with me and have to rely on my memory only, and all his knowledge would be of such great help to me who have so little.

And then I miss you all as well, and should like to have you close to me, dear faces which I kiss and which I love.

XV.
To MME. VICTOR HUGO.

BINGEN, 28*th September*, 1840.

Good-morning, my darling Adèle; my fondest love to you. I am now at Bingen. To-morrow I shall be at Mayence and I shall get your letters; I shall get letters from all of you, my beloved ones. It will be like seeing you all again. I am quite joyful. You and the others must write to Trèves in future. If time allows, I think of writing the same work on the Moselle, a beautiful and little known river, that I am now finishing on the Rhine.

"On the 14th of September *M. Jules Janin, author, and M. Victor Hugo, id.*, passed through Bingen," — the names are entered there in the visitors' book of the Victoria Hotel, by Jules Janin himself, whose handwriting I think I recognized. M. Victor Hugo, the landlord informs me, did not look very like his portraits, and had mustaches. The two gentlemen were in high spirits, and had three charming ladies with them. They made all the excursions in the neighborhood. Their arrival upset the whole town. They were very good fellows, however. The landlord asked me if I knew them. I said yes, slightly, but only by name. Now strangers are shown their names written in the visitors' book. It has made quite a stir in the little Roman town of Bingen, which, however, was once visited by Charlemagne. As for me, I travel quite incognito and unrecognized, and I am glad of it.

I hope to find nice letters from everybody at Mayence, and to hear that you are all well, and that the holidays, which, alas! are drawing to a close, have been well spent in much pleasure and a little work.

My darling Dédé, just now I hear a little girl of your age chattering in the room next mine, who reminds me of you, dear child. Be very good to your mother, your sister, and your brother, and your daddy will love you very much.

My Didine, my Charles, my Toto, I will write to each of you from Mayence, where I shall find all your letters. I send you all a thousand kisses, as well as to your dear mother, my children, my joy, my life. Think of me, and pray for me night and morning. You are continually in my thoughts.

My kind regards to your good father. I hope all my scribblings amuse and interest him, and that he will correct me when necessary.

One more kiss for you, dearest. You see there is room for it.

XVI.

To THE SAME.

MAYENCE, 1*st October*, 1840.

I ought to scold you, dearest, for having written me such a short letter. But as it was gentle and loving, I forgive you this time, on condition that it does not occur again, and that you will at any rate write me a good long letter to Trèves. You ought to understand that, after an absence which already seems very long to me, I want to hear a little of what is going on in Paris, or at all events at Saint-Prix. So write to me everything you hear about everything that you know will interest me. I believe some of our friends go to see you at Saint-Prix. Repeat to me what they tell you. Here are letters for all the children, for Julie, and for your good father. It was a great pleasure to me to hear that Julie was quite well.

Have you seen Mme. Menessier-Nodier? Have you even written to her? Have you asked her to the house? Do not forget, dearest, to pay some attentions in that quarter; they are friends of seventeen years' standing.

I am going to see Mannheim, Heidelberg, and Frankfort; then, if the weather holds up, I shall come down the Rhine and follow the course of the Moselle, as I have already told you. My next letter will bring you the continuation of my diary.

Here are a lot of drawings for the children. I have tried to divide them equally. Each child has an equal share of my heart.

I have been to Bingen, Rüdesheim, the famous Rat Tower. Just now I am exploring Mayence, a most interesting place. This journey will have been of great use to me, — and, I hope, to you all.

In conclusion, dearest, I remind you once more how much I hope to find at least one nice long letter from you at Trèves. Tell me if my diary interests you. You know that you and my beloved children are the sole object of my work in this world. Some day I shall leave you all the edifice that I shall have built.

I hope that my name will be a tower of strength to my children.

So write to me soon and often, my darling Adèle. I shall love you the more.

Your dear old HUSBAND.

XVII.

To TOTO.

MAYENCE, 1st October, 1840.

Here, my dear little Toto, is a sketch I have done for you. I am sending it directly after having read your nice dear little letter. A month hence, my darling, you will see your father again, and that will be as happy a day for him as for you.

When this letter reaches you, your holidays will be nearly at an end. You and my Charlie will both be returning to school, and, I trust, with renewed courage and fresh strength. All my hopes and all my happiness are centred in you, my dear ones. Your dear mother tells me she is satisfied with all of you. Make her as happy as she deserves, she who loves you so much, and who, like me, thinks only of you and your happiness in this world.

The child is father to the man; never forget this, my little Toto; be an industrious scholar, and I answer for it that you will one day be what is called a man, *vir*.

All the details you give me of your games and work have greatly interested me. When you have received this letter, write me a few lines to Trèves, and tell me a great deal more about yourself, your brother, and your sisters, and everything at home. This enables me to share in your pleasures, your amusements, your daily life; and I imagine that I am among you all, my darling children.

I am delighted to hear that all the animals belonging to my little shepherdess Dédé are quite well, and that you have finished your house of leaves and branches. Tell Dédé that she must write me rather a longer letter than the first.

As for me, my Toto, you will see, if you read my letters to your mother, that I am working, and that *even in my holidays* I try not to waste my time. I see beautiful countries, I study very novel and very curious things, but they are not worth your kisses and caresses, nor a couple of hours spent among you all at Saint-Prix.

So, my dear little Toto, go back to school bravely, work well, write to me, please your mother and your masters, and remember I am hardly a moment without thinking of you. Nothing of what I see diverts my mind from you, my children. All that I am and all that I do in this world is for you.

I love you, I love you dearly, my little Toto.

XVIII.

To BÉRANGER.

MAYENCE, 4th *October*, 1840.

I am at Mayence, a place which has been French, which will become French again one day, — which still is so in heart and mind, and will be until it is marked thus on the map by the red or blue line of the frontier. Just now I was at my window overlooking the Rhine. I was listening vaguely to the noise of the water-mills moored to the old sunken piles of Charlemagne's bridge, and thinking of the great things which Napoleon did here, when from a neighboring window a woman's voice, a sweet voice, wafted me snatches of the charming lines: —

> "J'aime qu'un russe soit russe,
> Et qu'un anglais soit anglais;
> Si l'on est prussien en Prusse,
> En France, soyons français.
>
> . . . . . .
> Mes amis! mes amis!
> Soyons de notre pays!
>
> . . . . . .
> Qui s'écriait à Pavie
> Tout est perdu fors l'honneur?
>
> . . . . . .
> Consolons par ce mot-là
> Ceux que le nombre accabla."

These noble lines of yours, heard in this way and in this spot, touched me deeply. I send you the fragments as they were borne to me on the breeze. They brought tears to my eyes, and I felt irresistibly impelled to write to you. My heart was sad in a place where a Frenchman ought not to be a foreigner; where a white soldier and a blue soldier, *i. e.*, Austria and Prussia, mount guard in front of the citadel defended in '94 by our people in Mayence, and enlarged by Napoleon in 1807. Your lines have gladdened my heart. This song of a woman is the protest of a whole people. I thought you would like to know that the Rhine reëchoes with your voice, and that the town of Frauenlob sings the songs of Béranger.

I am only passing through Mayence, but I am taking a deep impression away with me. I owe this to you, and I thank you for it. Dear great poet, I am your devoted admirer.

XIX.

To MME. VICTOR HUGO.

HEIDELBERG, *9th October*, 1840.

Here, dearest, is another large installment of my diary. I am afraid I may be obliged to give it up; for what with traveling, or seeing buildings, or studying in libraries in the daytime, I can write only at night. Sometimes I spend the whole night over it, and my eyes suffer in consequence. Still, as I fancy it interests your father, and amuses you all a little, I shall do my best to go on with it. Besides, it is a useful work, inasmuch as a number of local things, which are in danger of being lost or obliterated, are recorded in it for the first time. Well, I shall try to make my eyes serve me, though I cannot be very sure of them. Your father will find in this letter some unpublished details of the coronation of the emperors at Frankfort, which I fancy he will think curious.

I have calculated that you ought to have received my last letters on Sunday. That day my thoughts were constantly with you all, my beloved ones. Those of you who did not care for their drawings have only to tell me so, and I will make them others in Paris.

I hope, dearest, that all is still going on well. The rumors of war which penetrate here do not, I think, reach Saint-Prix.

By this time you will have lost Charlie and Toto. The dear children have doubtless gone back to M. Jauffret. You must impress on them from me, dearest, that I expect them to persevere in their studies.

I shall set to work, too, on my return. It is important that this winter should be a productive and fruitful one for me, and I hope we shall both succeed in making it so, you by economy and I by work.

In about three weeks I shall see you all again. It will be a happy day for me, and for you also I hope, my Adèle.

My darling Adèle, my beloved Didine, remember that I expect to find several letters from you both at Trèves, and that I must have them. And from you too, my little Dédé. If Charlie and Toto can write to me, in spite of their lessons, they will give their papa a great deal of pleasure. I hope, also, to get a letter from your good father, to whom I send my kindest regards. We shall soon meet again, my darlings. A thousand kisses to you all.

XX.

To THE SAME.

STOCKART, 19*th October*, 1840.

I am writing to you, dearest, in the midst of the grandest storm imaginable. I am in the Black Forest, and I am going to see Schaffhausen to complete my Rhine tour. I inclose the beginning of a letter to Boulanger,[1] whose address I have forgotten. You may all read it at Saint-Prix, if you like; after that, put the sheets in an envelope and send them to Louis.

It is rainy in the Moselle country, so I have given up going there. I shall return to Heidelberg to see the interior of the Black Forest; and from there I shall come straight into France by Forbach. Write

[1] An artist of merit, a friend of Victor Hugo.

to me now (and pray do so, dearest, as soon as you have received this) a nice little letter to Forbach, *poste restante* (France). I wrote to the post-office at Trèves to have all your letters sent on there. I shall find them as I pass through.

In a few days you will receive the conclusion of the letter to Boulanger. That will serve as a sort of continuation of my diary for Heidelberg, which is a delightful spot.

I live in the thoughts of you all, and in hopes that everything is going on well at Saint-Prix. I hope you are in good health, and that my dear children give you no trouble.

Just now I am passing through a lovely country. Before long, perhaps, it will be devastated by war. When I see a ruin I observe it carefully. Perhaps it will be used as a military position, and in another year I should not be able to recognize it.

My eyes still give me trouble; but I spare them. I must do so, for they will have to work this winter.

A few more days, and then I shall embrace you, my Adèle. I hope by the 1st of November I shall have that happiness.

Please write me *a long letter* to Forbach, and give me the latest news of you all. If you only knew how I long for it! Farewell, my beloved; that is to say, good-by for the present only.

When you see them, kiss my two dear little schoolboys, Charlie and Toto, for me.

XXI.

To Chateaubriand.

December, 1840.

Five and twenty years have passed, and there remain only great things and two great men, Napoleon and Chateaubriand. Permit me to lay these lines[1] at your feet. You have long ago made peace with the illustrious shade who inspired them.

Let me offer them to you as a fresh token of my old and profound admiration.

XXII.

To Savinien Lapointe.[2]

March, 1841.

Dear Sir, — If your lines were only beautiful, I might perhaps be less moved by them, but they are noble ones. I am more than charmed, — I am touched. Continue your twofold office, your task as a workman, and your mission as a thinker. You speak to the people as one of themselves, others address them from an elevation; your eloquence is not the least efficacious; your lot is a good one, believe me.

Courage, then, and patience! Courage for the great sorrows of life, and patience for the small ones. And then when you have laboriously accomplished your daily task, go to sleep in peace. God is awake.

I believe in God, and I believe in humanity. God sets a goal at the end of every path. All we have to do is to advance.

---

[1] *Le retour de l'empereur.*
[2] Savinien Lapointe was a shoemaker and a poet.

Always follow the grave and mysterious monitions of your conscience. I have said in one of my works, and I think it more than ever: *The poet has the care of souls.* In the profound darkness which still envelops so many minds, men like you among the people are the torches which light the work of others. Endeavor to increase unceasingly the quantity and the purity of your light.

XXIII.
To CHARLES DE LACRETELLE.

PARIS, 10*th June*, 1841.

I have just left, my venerable friend, the first private meeting of the Academy at which I have been present, and I find your letter on my return. I will not delay a moment in answering it. It charms me as everything does which comes from you. You know how to impart your feelings to your style. Everything you write has a fragrance of the soul.

I am glad that my speech [1] is so highly thought of at Bel-Air. It represents simply the honest convictions of a man who has no personal interest in the questions of the day, who is devoted above all things to civilization, to thought, and to his country. To have found an echo in your heart is glory for me.

Go on, my dear good colleague, love those who love you, and write for those who understand you.

[1] His speech on the occasion of his reception by the Academy.

XXIV.

To Alphonse Karr.

20th June, 1841.

My dear Alphonse Karr,[1] — You are poetry incarnate which complains of a poet and is right.

I, on my side, am not wrong. I have something of the poet, but a great deal of the soldier. As you remark so wittily, Salvandy's speech was emptied over my head, but after all, I have got the seat! and you are there too, and so are all my ideas and yours.

After all, the Academy has been a great institution, and can and should become so again, thanks to all the thoughtful and promising men of whom I am but the henchman, thanks to the real poets and the genuine writers. It contains, even at the present moment, worthy men who love you and who will welcome you; Academies, like everything else, will belong to the coming generation.

In the mean while, I am the living gap by which these ideas enter to-day, and through which these men will pass to-morrow.

That, I can imagine, is of small importance to you just now, who are living face to face with the ocean, with nature, and with God; but fall back towards us a little; turn your thoughts from great Etretat to little Paris; don't you think that we must be somewhat tired of being governed in literature by M. Roger, and in politics by M. Fulchiron?

I too love you, and most sincerely, for you have a noble heart and a noble mind.

---

[1] In *Les Guêpes* Alphonse Karr had blamed Victor Hugo for wishing to get into the Academy.

Scold Gatayes for me; he has been of infinite service to me, and now neglects me, ungrateful man!

XXV.
To Pierre Vinçard.

2d *July*, 1841.

Dear Sir, — As you do me the honor of sending me your article,[1] I take it as a letter, and answer it. I did not say "la *populace*;" I said "les *populaces.*" This plural is of importance: there is a gilded populace as well as a ragged one; there is a populace in drawing-rooms as well as in the streets.

In every stratum of society, the working, the thinking, the helpful element, that which aspires to goodness, justice, and truth, constitutes the people; that which is sunk in voluntary stagnation, which is ignorant from laziness, which does wrong willingly, is the populace.

In the upper ranks, selfishness and idleness; in the lower ones, envy and sloth, — that is the life of the populace; and, I repeat it, there is a populace in the upper ranks as well as the lower ones. I therefore said that we must love the people; a more severe moralist might perhaps have added, and *hate* the populace. I confined myself to despising it.

But, dear sir, I do not despise the complaint of a sterling and honest man, even when it is ill-founded; I try to enlighten him; it is a sacred duty for me. You see that I endeavor to discharge it.

---

[1] The subject of the article was Victor Hugo's speech on his reception into the Academy.

XXVI.

To THE KEEPER OF THE ARCHIVES ISRAELITES.[1]

SAINT-MANDE, 11*th June*, 1843.

You have misunderstood me, dear sir, and I greatly regret it, for it would be a real grief to me to have pained a man like you, of so much worth, learning, and character. The dramatic poet is also a historian, and he can no more alter history than human nature. Now the thirteenth century is a period of twilight; it has deep shadows, very little light, violence, crime, innumerable superstitions, and great barbarousness, everywhere. The Jews were barbarous, so were the Christians; the Christians were the oppressors, the Jews were the oppressed; the Jews retaliated. What else could be expected? It is the natural action of every compressed spring and oppressed people. The Jews therefore revenged themselves in secret; legend or history, the story of the little Saint-Werner child proves it. Rumor, however, was worse than the truth; popular report exaggerated the facts; hatred invented and slandered, as it always does; this is probable, indeed, certain, but what is to be done? One must describe periods as they were: they were superstitious, credulous, ignorant, barbarous; one must follow their superstitions, their credulity, their ignorance, their barbarousness. The poet cannot help it; he simply says: *It is the thirteenth century*, and this hint should be enough.

Is that equivalent to saying that in the present day Jews kill and eat little children? Why, dear sir, in

---

[1] About the play of *Les Burgraves,* in which there is mention of a child which the Jews are supposed to have stolen to kill on their Sabbath.

these days Jews like you are full of learning and enlightenment, and Christians like me are full of esteem and regard for Jews like you. So extend your forgiveness to *Les Burgraves,* dear sir, and accept my sincere regards.

XXVII.

To MME. VICTOR HUGO, *at Havre.*

PARIS, *Tuesday,* 18*th July,* 1843.

I did right, dearest, in leaving Havre last Monday, for the bills were already overdue, and I had great difficulty in getting my money. I was obliged to put off my departure, and I spent a week in most tiresome negotiations. At last I have succeeded, and I am free to start, which I shall do at once.

None the less I am truly sad when I think of the week which I might have spent with you, my beloved Adèle, in the midst of my dear little colony at Havre, and which I was obliged to sacrifice to this paltry sum of six or seven hundred francs. The small annoyances of life are often real troubles. And this is one of them.

I was so happy all that day I spent at Havre! — so completely and perfectly happy! I saw you all full of beauty, life, joy, and health![1] I felt I was loved in that radiant circle. You looked your very best, and were kind, sweet, and charming to me. My warmest thanks to you for it.

I have been seeing Charlie almost every day this week. I shall see him again shortly. He is just now in for his examination (Latin prose), which he entered

---

[1] Victor Hugo was never to see his daughter Léopoldine again; she was drowned at Villequier, while he was traveling.

as head of his class. I am very pleased with him. We spent Sunday together at Mme. de Villeneuve's, who was delightful, and spoke of you in the warmest and most feeling manner. It was the fête of Maisons. Charles enjoyed it very much. I was sad amid all this enjoyment. I could not help comparing this Sunday with the last, and thinking how sweet, happy, and full that one was.

In a month Charlie will be at your side; in two months I shall be with you all. I wish these two months were over. But I really need this journey. Good-by, my darling Adèle; I will let you know soon where to write to me.

XXVIII.

To THE SAME.

COGNAC, 2d *September*, 1843.

I am sending you a few lines, dearest, in great haste. For the last week I have been traveling night and day without stopping or taking any rest. I have left the Pyrenees, I have been to Tarbes, Auch, Agen, Bergerac, Périgueux, Angoulême, Jarnac, and I am going to Saintes, then to La Rochelle, where I hope to find nice letters from you and from the others, my dear ones. I am writing to you alone this time, for my eyes are sore from the dust and glare of the roads; and besides, I know what I write to you is for all, — you are the mother. So this letter is for everybody, as it is for you.

At Luz I received a nice little letter from my darling Didine.[1] As usual, it was full of love and happiness.

---

[1] She died on the 4th of September.

And I also got one from dear old Charlie. This year has not come up to our hopes and his work; he must pluck up fresh courage for next year. People of spirit may be eclipsed for a time, but cannot disappear altogether! So you must come to the front again, do you see, dear Charlie. In the mean while, enjoy yourself. And you too, my darling Toto, and you, my little pet Dédé. School-time is approaching; make the most of the holidays.

I shall be with you shortly. In about a fortnight I shall be embracing you all, and we shall be together again. I will tell you all my *adventures.* You will tell me, as you used to do when you all four sat together on my knees, all your thoughts, your joys, your wishes. My Toto will ask me a hundred questions, and I will give him twice as many answers. Take care of yourself, Toto.

Dearest, as I am returning so soon, my letters will not be so frequent; do not be surprised at this. Writing is but a poor substitute; what I want is to embrace you and have you all.

So good-by for the present only, my beloved ones.

XXIX.

To MLLE. LOUISE BERTIN, *at Les Roches.*

SAUMUR, 10*th September*, 1843.

DEAR MADEMOISELLE LOUISE, — I am suffering, I am heart-broken; my turn has come, you see. I feel I must write to you, — you who loved her[1] like a second mother; you know, too, how fond she was of you.

---

[1] His daughter Léopoldine.

Yesterday I had just taken a long hot walk over the marshes; I was tired and thirsty; I came into a village called, I think, Subise, and went into a café. They brought me a glass of beer and a paper, the *Siècle*. I read the news. It was thus that I learnt that the best part of my life and of my affections was dead.

I loved that poor child more than words can tell. You remember how charming she was. She was the sweetest, the most winning of creatures.

O God, in what have I offended thee? She was too fortunate; she had everything: beauty, intelligence, youth, love. This perfect happiness made me tremble; I put up with my separation from her in order that something might be lacking to her. There should always be a cloud. This one was not enough. God will not allow us to have paradise on earth. He has taken her back. Oh, my poor darling! — to think I shall never see her again.

Forgive me; I write to you in despair. But it is some comfort to me. You are so kind, you have such a lofty character, you will understand me, I am sure. I am fondly attached to you, and when I suffer, I fly to you.

I shall arrive in Paris almost at the same time as this letter. My poor wife and children sadly need me.

My kindest regards to you,
VICTOR HUGO.

My love to kind Armand. May God keep him, and may he never suffer as I do now.

XXX.

To LOUIS BOULANGER.

SAUMUR, 10*th September*, [1843].

DEAR LOUIS, — I began a long letter to you, and I am sending you a few lines. You will understand. I write to you in the depths of despair. You are my friend, and I must make you share this grief with me. God has taken away the very light of our life and of our home. Oh, my poor child, my poor darling, she was too happy. I was right, then, in my thoughts which so often dwelt on her, to be frightened at so much happiness. Dear Louis, love me. I am hurrying to Paris, but I wanted to write to you. Alas! I am broken-hearted.

XXXI.

To VICTOR PAVIE.

PARIS, 17*th September*, [1843].

I no longer live, my dear friend, I no longer think; I suffer; my eyes are fixed on heaven; I wait.

What beautiful and touching things you say to me! Hearts like yours understand everything because they contain everything. Alas! what an angel I have lost!

Be happy! be blest! My blessing must be acceptable to God, for in his kingdom the poor are rich and the wretched great.

My fondest love to you.

XXXII.

To Alphonse Karr,[1] at Sainte-Adresse.

Paris, 18th September, 1843.

You have drawn tears from me at this dreadful time; you have harrowed me and relieved me; thanks, dear, noble Alphonse Karr. You have a great heart; you have spoken appropriately of her and of him. My poor dear child! Can you realize that I shall never see her again?

XXXIII.

To Edouard Thierry.

23d September, 1843.

We have both received a blow almost at the same time, — you in the loss of your brother, I in that of my daughter. What can you say to me, and what can I say to you? Let us weep together, let us hope together. Death has its revelations, — the great sorrows which open the heart open the mind as well; light comes to us with our grief. As for me, I have faith; I believe in a future life. How could I do otherwise? My daughter was a soul; I saw this soul; I touched it, so to speak. It was with me for eighteen years; my eyes are still full of its radiance; even in this world she visibly belonged to the life above. I suffer as you do; hope as I do.

---

[1] Alphonse Karr had hurried from Sainte-Adresse to Villequier, and had written a touching account of the death of Léopoldine and her husband, Charles Vacquerie, in *Les Guêpes*.

XXXIV.

To CHARLES DE LACRETELLE.

PARIS, 9*th July*, 1844.

Your excellent letter, my dear and venerable friend, has done me more good than I can tell you. In the deep melancholy in which I am plunged, the contemplation of an old man's soul, beautiful, strong, and serene as yours, is a great help to bearing my life. It is comforting and useful to us younger men, who are afflicted and tried by Providence, to let our thoughts rest on your white hairs, on your mature wisdom. You, too, have lived, struggled, and suffered. Where I have wounds, you have scars. Now you are calm, contented, resigned, and happy, and you gaze mildly at the majestic region whence come all the rays which give light to our eyes, and all the misfortunes which illumine our souls. For nothing is more true than that misfortune brings understanding. How many things have I seen in myself and outside myself since my sorrow! The highest hopes spring from the deepest griefs. Let us thank God for having given us the right to suffer, since it brings with it the right to hope.

As for you, my good and venerable friend, you are happy already, even in this world. Your beautiful and noble old age participates in the joys promised to the elect. What can a blessed eternity give you better than the noble and charming wife who loves and admires you, than the gentle, amiable, and noble children whom you make happy, and who make you happy? God is just. He has begun your Paradise on earth; for you death will be a continuation of it.

XXXV.

To Victor Pavie.[1]

[*November*, 1844.]

Alas! what a sad echo your heart awakens in mine! Like me, you are face to face with the great sorrow of your life. To see one's flower wither, one's future destroyed, one's hopes turned into despair! Alas! I could not have wished such a thing for my worst enemy! why does Providence send this anguish to one of my best and dearest friends? Let us repeat the grand words: *In a better land!*

My respects to the poor mother. V.

XXXVI.

To Théophile Gautier.

[1845.]

Do you remember, my friend, what an outcry there was when — it was toward the end of the Restoration — some one you know took it into his head one fine day, in some paper or other, and apropos of some discussion or other on art in the Middle Ages, to put forth, in the presence of all the shaven chins of France and Europe, a clear, explicit, and formal profession of faith, without ambiguity or reserve, in favor of the beard?

God, he said, if my memory serves me, — God wished to make, and has made, the head of man beautiful. He raised the forehead to give room for the intelligence; He kindled the glance under the arch of the eyebrow,

[1] On the death of his young daughter, Elizabeth Pavie.

as a lamp shining in the deep and mysterious cavern of thought; He placed pride, disdain, and passion in the open and mobile nostril, grace in the expressive and smiling mouth, dignity in the transparent and calm cheeks, serenity and reflection in the prominent and well-cut chin; and on the whole countenance He stamped the serenity and strength of a nature which knows and understands itself. But this head of man, of Adam, which God has made beautiful, society tends to make ugly. Society, civilization, the whole group of complicated and necessary phenomena due to the healthy and normal labor of the mind and to the aberrations of moral liberty, leave their mark on the human face. The calculations of interest take the place of the speculations of the intellect; when the inmate dwindles in size the house shrinks; so the brow becomes narrow and low. When interest has superseded intelligence, pride disappears, the nostril contracts; the eye grows dull, — the pupil remains, but the expression is gone; the glass is there, but not the lamp. The nose is crushed, becomes flat or prominent, and has a tendency to get farther from the mouth as in the animal, a distressing sign of stupidity. A number of infirmities and complaints incidental to civilization and unknown in a state of nature — for animals never have anything the matter with their jaws — attack the mouth, wither the lips, blacken the teeth, and poison the breath. The eye has just lost its expression, the mouth loses its smile. Finally, the chin becomes shapeless and retires into the background; for in the line of the human profile the chin follows the fortunes of the forehead, of which it is, at the bottom of the face, the expressive complement, advancing when the forehead is developed, retreating when it contracts, — a melancholy and humiliating transformation which inevitably goes on from generation to generation. But God had foreseen this transformation. This ugliness, bred of civilization, which in course of time overlays the beauty of the natural man, God wished from the beginning to palliate and hide, and for that purpose He gave to man, the very day on which He created him, that splendid mask of folly,[the beard.] What a number of things, in fact, are concealed by the beard, to the great advantage of the human face: the sunken cheeks, the retreating chin, the faded lips, the contracted nostrils, the distance from the nose to the mouth, the toothless gums, the smile which has lost its charm. Substitute for all these horrors, some of which are plagues and others ridiculous, a rich and splendid growth which frames and fills out the face by continuing the hair of the head, and mark the effect. Equilibrium is reëstablished, beauty returns. The moral is that a man's head must indeed be beautiful, modeled by intelligence and illumined by thought, to be beautiful without a beard; that a human face must indeed be ugly, irredeemably disfigured by pettiness and vulgarity, to be ugly with a beard. Therefore, let your beards grow, all ye who are ugly and who wish to be handsome !

When the writer in question had penned these bold and memorable words, like the brave and gallant man that he is, he did not retreat; he did not flinch. Another man, foreseeing, as he foresaw it, the storm about to break over his head, might, perhaps, have preferred repose to glory, and thrown the pages into the fire. He, seeing them written, thought they were to the point and worth publishing, and like an honest man who takes a serious step, he signed them. But, whatever may have been his expectation, the event surpassed it. The matter was even more serious than he had supposed. You shoot at a sparrow, and kill a partridge. He imagined he had only made a profession of faith. He had issued a proclamation. When this audacious and shameless declaration appeared, you recollect, my friend, what a grand hubbub there was! what a frightful battle! what a glorious row! what a magnificent uproar! The war of the chins against the beards broke out. For twelve long months the noise in the papers was deafening.

Every question — the Greek question, the Balkans question, the Neapolitan question, the Eastern question, the Spanish question — disappeared in a flood of pamphlets and articles, under the beard question. A few young artists, painters, sculptors, and musicians, intrepid and intelligent pioneers of every idea, had the courage to put the theory into practice, and left off shaving. Then came a fresh deluge of prose, verse, satire, ballads, couplets, and caricatures. The rain turned into hail. When the bearded ones passed by on the boulevards or the street crossings, women turned away their heads, old men raised their eyes to heaven, the street urchins hooted *the man with a beard*. There were pen-duels and sword-duels. Fighting exasperated the combatants; their bile rose, and for the space of a whole year *they sneezed epigrams*, as Piron says.

Providence was severely taken to task for having invented beards. The man adorned with this appendage was called a goat. The beard was declared to be ugly, foolish, dirty, filthy, foul, repulsive, ridiculous, unpatriotic, Jewish, frightful, abominable, hideous, and, what was then the *ne plus ultra* of abuse, romantic!

All the diseases of the scalp were raked up, — the plica of the Poles, the leprosy of the Hebrews, the mentagra of the Romans. It was said that with the beard the variety of the human physiognomy would disappear; that all faces would be alike; that there would be only four types of head left, — the dark, the fair, the gray, and the red; that when this came to pass man would be hideous in the eyes of woman, and that Adam with a beard would be so ill-favored that Eve would not look at him. It was said that a really handsome man would never have recourse to this expedient of hiding half of his face, and that the only really fine heads were those which could do without a beard. It was said that never would one of the great rulers of the world, with his Roman profile, laurel-girt brow, deep-set eyes, and imperial cheeks, have dreamed of hiding his projecting chin, with its severe and pensive beauty, under a mass of hair; and that every emperor, from Cæsar down to Napoleon, had shaved his chin.

From the outset the shrill-voiced and venerable school which upholds "sound doctrines," "taste," the "grand age," "the tender Racine," etc., etc., etc., had intervened in the dispute. It had pronounced the beard romantic; it declared the shaven chin classic. After a year of rage and fury, it proclaimed its victory by asserting in a triumphant and absolute manner that never would France, never would "the most intelligent people in the world," adopt the odious fashion of letting the beard grow.

Fifteen years have passed. The same thing has happened which always befalls the victories of the classic school. Nowadays everybody in France wears a beard.

Everybody,— except, perhaps, the man who started this grand quarrel and achieved this great success.

XXXVII.

To The Editor of the Phare de la Loire.

1845.

You think I am a rich man, dear sir? Listen to this. I have been working for twenty-eight years, for I began when I was fifteen. During those twenty-eight years I have earned about five hundred thousand francs by my pen. I inherited nothing from my father; my stepmother and the lawyers kept what there was. I might have brought an action, but against whom? Against a person who bore my father's name. I preferred to submit to spoliation. For eight and twenty years I have not rested for two consecutive months. I have educated my four children. M. Villemain offered me scholarships for my sons, and the St. Denis school for my daughters. I refused, as I was in a position to educate my children at my own expense, and I did not wish to saddle the State with what I could pay myself.

To-day, of these five hundred thousand francs there remain three hundred thousand. These three hundred thousand francs I have invested, — capitalized, as they say, — and I do not touch them, for I have worked too hard to live to be old, and I do not want my wife and children to receive pensions when I am dead. I live on the interest. I still write, which increases my income a little, and I support eleven persons, — all liabilities and charges included. Add eighty-three francs a month as member of the Institute, which I was forgetting. I owe no one anything. I have never made a traffic of anything. I spend a little in charity, — as much as I can. Those around me want for nothing. As for myself, I wear overcoats which cost twenty-five francs, I wear my hats rather too long, I work without a fire in winter, and I go to the Chamber[1] on foot.

I am grateful, however. I have always possessed the two blessings without which I could not live, — a tranquil conscience and complete independence.

XXXVIII.

To Arsène Houssaye.

6th February, 1847.

Madame Victor Hugo has told me of the terrible blow which has just befallen you. My dear poet, I send you, as well as the poor mother, my warmest and deepest sympathy. I know too well what suffering is to be able to console. You have lost the angel of the house, — the flower, the joy, the sweet spring of life! Alas! I have experienced the same calamity. You will issue from it as I have done; life falls into its old groove because God wills it.

We are the slaves of destiny and thought. We go

---

[1] Victor Hugo had been raised to the *Chambre des Pairs* by Louis Philippe on the 13th of April, 1845.

hither and thither, we work, we even smile; but, whatever we do, there is always a sad and sombre thing in the heart, — the memory of the departed child. God help you, dear poet! I can only give you my hand, and bow my head to your affliction as to my own.

XXXIX.

To LAMARTINE.

24th March, 1847.

Incedo per ignes. All that I have read of your book[1] is magnificent. Here at last is the Revolution treated by a historian on a footing of equality. You apprehend these giants; you grasp these huge events with ideas which are on a par with them. They are immense; but you are great.

Occasionally, however, for the good of the just and holy popular cause which we love and which we both serve, I could wish that you were more severe. You are so strong that you can be, you are so noble that you ought to be. But I am dazzled with the book, and delighted with its success.

XL.

To THE SAME.

Sunday, 27th February, [1848].[2]

DEAR AND ILLUSTRIOUS FRIEND, — I had gone to greet you in the public square while you came to my house to shake me by the hand. I return you your greeting.

You are doing great things. The abolition of capital punishment, this signal lesson given by a newly born

---

[1] *Histoire des Girondins.*   [2] After the Revolution of 1848.

Republic to the old time-honored monarchies, is a grand achievement.

I applaud with hands and heart.

You have the genius of the poet, the genius of the writer, the genius of the orator; you have wisdom and courage. You are a great man.

I admire you and love you.

XLI.

To MME. VICTOR HUGO.

24*th June*, [1848].[1]
FROM THE ASSEMBLY,[2] 8 *o'clock in the morning.*

DEAREST,—I spent the night at the Assembly, awaiting events. This morning, at six, I tried to join you and embrace you all in the Place Royale. I managed to get as far as the Hôtel de Ville by way of the quay, through a few volleys of musketry. I spoke to General Duvivier, and pushed on to the entrance of the Rue Saint-Antoine. Here, on the Place Baudoyer, there were barricades guarded by troops of the line. Shots were being exchanged. The officers implored me not to go further, and a representative who came up pointed out to me that if I did so I ran the risk of falling into the hands of the insurgents, who might perhaps keep me as a hostage, which would embarrass the Assembly. I turned back, in great distress, and very anxious about my dear Place Royale. All the National Guards, and a professor at the Charlemagne College who was on the barricade, assured me that the Place Royale was

---

[1] The first day of the insurrection.

[2] Victor Hugo had been elected a member of the *Assemblée Constituante* on the 4th of June, 1848.

quiet. I hope that by this evening the road will be free, and that you will see me again; my thoughts are with you all.

What a terrible thing! and how sad to think that all this blood shed on both sides is that of brave and generous men! Tell Charles not to run too many risks. Let him do his duty, as I do mine, but avoid all imprudence.

We are sitting permanently; the Assembly will resume work in a few minutes.

XLII.

To MME. VICTOR HUGO.

25th June, [1848], *a quarter to nine.*

Here is the news. The situation is serious. To-day's fighting will be fiercer than yesterday's. The number of the insurgents has increased. Troops from the suburbs and fresh regiments have arrived. All the National Guards within a radius of sixty leagues are on the move and coming to defend Paris.

It is thought, however, that the events of to-day will be decisive. But what a sad ending for so many honest fellows killed on both sides!

Bixio was shot in the chest yesterday, and Dornès in the groin. Both are dying. Clément Thomas and Bedeau are wounded. And then so many worthy National Guards! And the poor misguided workmen! We have just decreed that the Republic shall provide for the widows and orphans.

Do not be anxious, dearest. All will be well. Calm my Dédé. I embrace you all with a sad heart.

XLIII.

To THE SAME.

[*26th June*, 1848.[1]]

DEAREST, — I am in terrible anxiety. Where are you? What has become of you? For two days I have been prowling day and night in your neighborhood without being able to get to you. I am tortured by suspense. Send me one line, just to say you are all safe and well. I can hardly breathe. Give me full accounts of everybody.

I have been here for the last four and twenty hours with a mandate of order, peace, and conciliation.[2] God is helping and will help us. France will be saved.

Above all, be easy on my account. I am well, though worn out with fatigue.

XLIV.

To CHARLES DE LACRETELLE.

FROM THE ASSEMBLY, 1*st July*, 1848.

We are all safe and sound, my dear old friend. God did not want my life, for I gladly risked it to arrest this disastrous effusion of French blood. I write to you in haste from the vortex called the Assembly. My wife sends her best love to yours. We are moving to-day. In future write to me at No. 5, Rue d'Isly. My kindest regards to yourself.

---

[1] Written in pencil.

[2] Victor Hugo was one of the commissioners appointed by the Assembly on the 24th of June to make known to the population of Paris the steps which had been taken. On the 24th and 25th of June he had been at the barricades, haranguing the insurgents.

XLV.

To ULRIC GÜTTINGUER.

FROM THE ASSEMBLY, 10*th July*, 1848.

DEAR ULRIC,— we are out of the fray, but still in the uproar. I think of you among your trees and flowers, and I write to you. You witness the tempests of the ocean; I see storms of another kind, and I envy you.

But let us take heart. It is impossible that civilization should collapse, but humanity must make an effort. The wound is deep and dangerous, but who dare say to the Supreme Healer, Thou canst not cure it?

For my part, I hope. I hoped during the insurrection, under a storm of bullets; I continued to hope, when I knew my family was in the power of the insurgents. I trusted in God. Not a shot touched me, not one of my family came to harm.

Dear poet, dear thinker, it is not necessary to teach charity, love, and faith to you. I am only repeating your own maxims. Yes, the new preachers of pillage and robbery are execrable, but the people is good.

Oh! how I long to be near you, amid nature, with my family, with yours! Alas! I am grinding here at the fatal revolutionary mill. I shall perhaps be among the first to be crushed by it, but I wish it to crush a heart full of confidence and love. V.

XLVI.

To LAMARTINE.

July, 1848.

MY ILLUSTRIOUS FRIEND,— You have treated my son as I should have treated yours. You spontaneously placed him near your person, you made him one of your private secretaries, and you loaded him with all the kindness your great heart could dictate. I thank you most warmly. The time which he spent with you will be one of the proudest moments of his life.

On leaving office, you offered to make my son an attaché to the Brazilian Legation. I now learn that the execution of your plan has met with an unexpected obstacle, and that M. Bastide, the Minister for Foreign Affairs, has democratic scruples about me and demurs to my name. Allow me to put an end to this hesitation in the only suitable way possible. I am writing to the Minister for Foreign Affairs to-day to beg him not to appoint my son.

My son is returning to the Minister at the same time his nomination for diplomatic employment. He will keep what was most precious about it in his eyes, the recollection of having received it from you.

I press your hand, dear Lamartine, and I renew the assurance of my profound admiration and long-standing friendship.

XLVII.

To CHARLES DE LACRETELLE.

FROM THE ASSEMBLY, 13*th February*, [1849].

You look on affairs, my venerable friend, with the clear and quiet glance of minds accustomed to contemplation and reflection. Men like you begin by judging and end by loving. As he grows old the historian softens and becomes a philosopher. Even your severity bears the stamp of kindness. You do not condemn things because you understand men.

But this placid serenity in no way detracts from

your warm-heartedness, and when our errors and follies deserve reprobation, your censure weighs all the more heavily on bad men because it proceeds from an indulgent mind.

The history which we are making does not deserve a historian like you. So I congratulate you on spending your life quietly at home in meditation and the composition of poetry. But send me, who am in the fight, a word of encouragement from time to time. The battle is not yet over. We who are in the thick of the fray still need strength and determination. As for me, my heart is divided between fear and hope. I have profound faith in the future of civilization and of France, but I do not hide from myself what the storm may bring. We may founder, as we may reach the land; I believe in two possibilities: a fearful shipwreck, a splendid port. May God conduct us! but let us help God.

XLVIII.

To GUSTAVE D'EICHTAL.

26th October, 1849.

The ideas which are in your mind are in mine too. I even go further. But is it possible in these days to say everything at once? When the flame is low, too much oil puts out the lamp. There are things which must not be mentioned, gleams of light which must be veiled, prospects which must be concealed, future realities which would be chimeras for the present age. Man cannot bear nudity in any form, the nudity of the future no more than any other. This luminous nudity would dazzle him. The reason is that he long ago lost, and is only slowly recovering, the feeling for and the love of the ideal.

We must all labor to restore him this feeling for and love of the ideal. We must not despair; quite the reverse. We have already lifted a corner of the veil in the Peace Congress. I tried to raise another in the debate on Rome. Little by little light breaks in, and, thanks to the courageous efforts of those who think, our age, at first so incredulous and ironical, begins to get accustomed to the brightness of the future.

You belong to those who decipher this great unknown, which is dark for the weak and radiant for the strong. You belong to those who affirm and hope. I rejoice to feel, like you, full of faith, that is, full of love. The ultra-Catholics of our day have no faith, and the proof of it is that they are full of hatred. Their eyes are blinded, and their hearts are turned to stone. Let us pity them, and let us pray to God that the great destinies of mankind may be accomplished soon enough to make them, in spite of themselves, happy and confident.

XLIX.

To HENRI DE LACRETELLE.

FROM THE ASSEMBLY,[1] 3*d June,* 1850.

Thanks, dear poet. What a good comforting message you sent me! The contest is keen, the enemy is full of ardor, hatred is bellowing its loudest, but how sweet is your greeting in the midst of the tumult! At this moment, while I am writing to you, I hear the bark of the Right; my thoughts go out to yours through all this uproar, and I seem to feel the gentle influence of your serenity.

[1] The *Assemblée Législative,* to which Victor Hugo had been elected in 1849.

How blest you are among your flowers and trees, with the conversation of your good father, with the smiles of your charming wife! You have nature, poetry, love, happiness. *We* have the spectacle of rage in the Senate, and disgrace in the laws. How mean and petty is the moment through which we are passing. Happily, the age is great.

Write us some fine verses, send me some noble letters, and love me.

L.

To MICHELET.[1]

Saturday, 29th March, 1851.

I was deeply pained on Thursday, my dear and eloquent colleague, pained to hear such things said from the tribune, and pained to be unable to reply to them. An indisposition which I could not overcome kept me glued to my seat.

Freedom of thought has been gagged in your person, freedom of conscience has been cashiered in that of M. Jacques; philosophy, reason, history, law, the three great centuries of emancipation, the sixteenth, the seventeenth, and the eighteenth, have been gainsaid; the nineteenth has been defied; all this was cheered by the party which commands a majority, all this was upheld, explained, commented on, glorified, for the space of two hours, by one M. Giraud, who is, I am told, your colleague and mine at the Institut; all this was said and done by the Minister who represents education in France, in the tribune which instructs the world! I left the Chamber ashamed and indignant.

---

[1] Michelet's course of lectures at the Collège de France had been suspended by the Government.

I send you my protest; I should like to send it to all the noble and generous youths who love and admire you.

I congratulate you on being persecuted for the holy cause of the French Revolution and the human mind.

LI.

To Mrs. Maria Chapman.

12th May, 1851.

Madam, — You are good enough to believe that a word from me, in this sacred cause of emancipation, may have some influence on the great American people whom I love so deeply, and whose destinies are, in my opinion, linked to the mission of France. You wish me to make my voice heard. I do it at once, and will do so on every occasion.

I have hardly anything to add to your letter. I could indorse every line of it. Continue your sacred task. All great minds and good hearts are on your side.

I agree with you that it is impossible that the United States of America should not, within a certain time, before long, give up slavery. Slavery in such a country! Was there ever such a monstrous contradiction? It is barbarism installed in the very heart of a society the whole of which is the affirmation of civilization. Liberty in chains, blasphemy proceeding from the altar, the negro's fetters riveted to the pedestal of Washington's statue! It is unheard of. I go further: it is impossible. It is a phenomenon which will disappear of itself. The light of the nineteenth century is sufficient to dissolve it.

What! slavery legalized in the illustrious nation which for the last sixty years has demonstrated progress by its advance and liberty by its prosperity! Slavery in the United States! It is the duty of this great republic to set this bad example no longer. It is a disgrace, and she is not one of those that hang the head! It is not for young nations to harbor slavery when old ones are discarding it. What! slavery is to quit Turkey and remain in America! The pashas are turning it out, and the country of Franklin is to adopt it! No, a thousand times no!

There is an inflexible logic which develops more or less slowly, which fashions, which rectifies — after a mysterious pattern of which great minds have a glimpse and which is the ideal of civilization — mankind, facts, laws, manners, peoples; or, to express it better, under human institutions there are divine ones. Let all generous hearts take courage!

The United States must either give up slavery or give up liberty! They will not give up liberty! They must either give up slavery or the gospel. They will not give up the gospel!

Accept, madam, with my warmest adhesion to the cause, the homage of my respect.

LII.

To MONSIEUR PARTARRIEU-LAFOSSE, *Président of the Assize Court.*

5th June, 1851.

MONSIEUR LE PRÉSIDENT, — My son Charles Hugo has been cited to appear before the Assize Court of which you are the presiding judge, on Tuesday, the

10th of June, on a charge of having failed in the respect due to the laws, in an article [1] on the execution of the condemned criminal Montcharmont.[2]

My son desires to be defended by me, and I wish to defend him.

In accordance with section 295 of the Code of Criminal Procedure I apply to you for permission to do so.

Receive the assurance of my distinguished consideration.

LIII.

To ANGELO BROFFERIO.

PARIS, 7th August, 1851.

DEAR AND ELOQUENT COLLEAGUE, — I have been a long while answering your letter; but you know what a stormy time we have gone through. Last month the Republic, liberty, progress, all the principles and truths of the nineteenth century were called in question. For a whole week I had to stand in this great breach and repulse the furious assault of the past on the present and the future.

With God's help we have conquered. The old parties have beat a retreat, and the Revolution has gained all the ground which they have lost. You know all this good news already, but it is a pleasure to me to tell it to you again, to you, Brofferio, who carry the standard of the people and of liberty so high aloft and so proudly in the Parliament of Piedmont.

---

[1] The article was signed by Charles Hugo and published in the *Evénement*, the newspaper founded by Victor Hugo in 1848. Victor Hugo defended his son, and made a speech against capital punishment. The jury found Charles Hugo guilty, and the court sentenced him to six months' imprisonment and to pay a fine of 500 francs.

[2] A poacher, who had killed two gendarmes and a forester.

Dear colleague, — for we are colleagues; besides the mandate of our countries we have the mandate of humanity, — dear and eloquent colleague, I thank you for the courage with which you inspire me, I congratulate you on the progress which you are achieving, and I press your two hands in mine.

II. THE COUP D'ETAT. — LETTERS FROM BRUSSELS.
1851-1852.

[The *coup d'état* of the 2d of December breaks out. In the morning of that day Victor Hugo leaves his house in the Rue de la Tour d'Auvergne and joins the representatives of the Left for the twelve days' struggle related in *L'Histoire d'un crime*.

On the 4th, communications are still uninterrupted. He sends Mme. Victor Hugo the following note in pencil.]

I.
To Mme. Victor Hugo.

[4*th December*, 1851.]

Dearest, — I spent the night with an excellent friend of the Davidal family, M. de la Roellerie. Thank them warmly on my behalf. Yesterday evening I presided over the meeting of the Left. Nothing is hopeless. I am starting this morning for the Faubourg Saint-Antoine.

In God's keeping!

[Madame Victor Hugo was left without news for several days. Subsequently she received, through an indirect channel, under the name of Madame Rivière, the two following letters.]

II.

Sunday, 7th December, [1851].

My dear Friend, — M. Rivière was obliged to leave without bidding you good-by. He requests me to let you know this. He intends, however, to write to you himself as soon as he has a moment to spare, and it will be a pleasure to him to express all that he feels for you.

As he was unable to find the portress when he was leaving, he begs you to be so good as to give her from him a gratuity of five francs, which Mme. Rivière will repay you the first time you see her. Kindly tell Mme. Rivière that her husband is well, that he sends her, as well as his daughter and his sons, his fondest love, and that he will write to them all soon.

M. Rivière sends you his kindest regards.

Albert Durand.

M. Rivière begs you to show this letter to his wife.

III.

Monday, 8th December, [1851].

My dear Friend, — M. Rivière is in good health, but he found so much to do on his arrival that he cannot write to you yet.

He bids me do it in his stead, requesting you at the same time to let his wife and children know. In the present state of affairs a little more time will be required for business to revive; everything, however, may come right eventually.

Tell Mme. and Mlle. Rivière that M. Rivière sends them his best love and hopes to see them soon.

Your friend, Albert Durand.

IV.

To "Madame Rivière" (Mme. Victor Hugo).

Brussels, 12*th December*, [1851]. 7 a.m.

A line in haste, dearest. I am here. It was no easy matter. Write to me at the following address: M. Lanvin, Bruxelles, *poste restante*.

If you have any letters for me, keep them all, *and do not give them to any one*. I will let you know how you can send them to me later on.

I hope that you have seen our dear children again. Send me detailed news. Take good care of all my papers. What has happened at home?

My keys will be delivered to you. You will find the securities in a portfolio on the red box in my lacquered wardrobe (your father's). Take great care of them.

Collect and take the utmost care of everything in the chest at the side of my bed. They are diaries, — the only copies I have. In the covered chest near my table there are some things of great value. I commend them to you.

What I commend to you above all is to be of good heart. I know that you have a lofty, strong nature. Tell my beloved children that my heart is with them. Tell my little Adèle that I do not want her to get pale or thin. Let her be calm. The future belongs to the good.

My warmest greetings to our friends, — to Auguste, to Meurice,[1] to his charming wife. I close this letter at once, so that it may reach you to-day.

---

[1] Auguste Vacquerie and Paul Meurice were, at this moment, in the Conciergerie prison with Charles and François-Victor Hugo.

V.

To MME. VICTOR HUGO.

BRUSSELS, *Sunday, 14th [December,* 1851]. 3 P. M.

I open your letter, dearest, and answer it at once. Do not be uneasy. The *drawings*[1] are in safety. *I have them with me here,* and so I shall be able to go on with my work. I had put them into another portmanteau. I took them with me when I left Paris.

For twelve days I have been betwixt life and death, but I have not had a moment's uneasiness. I have been satisfied with myself. And then I know that I have done my duty, and that I have done it thoroughly. That is a source of satisfaction. I met with complete devotion from those around me. Sometimes my life was at the mercy of ten persons at once. A word might have ruined me, but it was never spoken.

I owe an immense deal to M. and Mme. de M——, whom I mentioned to you. It was they who saved me at the most critical moment. Pay a *very friendly* visit to Mme. de M——. She lives near you, at No. 2, Rue Navarin. Some day I will tell you all that they did for me. In the mean while you cannot show yourself too grateful to them. It was all the more meritorious on their part because they are in the other camp, and the service they rendered me *might have seriously compromised them.* Give them credit for all this, and be very nice to Mme. de M—— and her husband, who is the best of men. The mere sight of him will make you like him. He is another Abel.[2]

---

[1] By *drawings* Victor Hugo meant his manuscripts.
[2] Abel Hugo, the poet's son.

Send me detailed news of my dear children, of my daughter, who must have suffered much. Tell them all to write to me. The poor boys must have been very uncomfortable in prison, owing to the crowding. Has any fresh severity been practiced on them? Write to me about it. I know that you go to see them every day. Do you still dine with our dear colony?[1]

I am putting up here at the Hotel de la Porte-Verte, room No. 9. I have for neighbor a worthy and courageous refugee representative, Versigny. He has room No. 4. Our doors are close to each other. I lead the life of an anchorite. I have a tiny bed, two straw-bottomed chairs, and no fire. My total expenses amount to three francs a day, everything included. Versigny lives as I do.

Tell my Charles that he must become quite a man. In the days when I carried my life in my hand I thought of him. He might at any moment have become the head of the family, the support of you all. He must think of this.

Live sparingly. Make the money which I left you last a long time. I have enough in prospect to get on here for some months.

Yesterday I saw the Minister of the Interior, M. Ch. Rogier, who paid me a visit in the Rue Jean-Goujon twenty years ago. When I came in I said to him laughingly, "I have come to return your visit."

He was very cordial. I told him that I had a duty, to write the history of what has happened, at once and while it was fresh. As actor, eye-witness, and judge, I am the historian for it. *That I could not accept*

---

[1] The four prisoners in the Conciergerie.

any condition as to residence. That they might expel me if they chose. That, however, I should only publish this *historical* work on condition of its not aggravating the condition of my sons, who are in the man's power at this moment. He might torture them, in fact.

Let me know your views. If anything from my pen can in any way inconvenience them, I will be silent. In that case I will confine myself to finishing my book *Les Misères* here. Who knows, perhaps this was the only chance of finishing it. We must never accuse or judge Providence. What a blessing, for instance, that my sons were in prison during the events of the 3d and the 4th!

M. Rogier told me that if I published this work now my presence might be a serious embarrassment to Belgium, — a small state with a powerful and overbearing neighbor. I said: "In that case, if I decide to publish it, I will go to London."

We parted good friends. He offered me some shirts. I certainly need some. I have no clothes nor linen. Take my empty portmanteau and put my things in it, — my new stocking trousers, my trousers that are not new, my old gray ones, my coat, my big frogged surtout, — the hood of which you will find on the carved bench, — and my new shoes. Besides the pair at home, I ordered another of Kuhn, my bootmaker, in the Rue de Valois, three weeks ago. Get them and pay for them (eighteen francs), and put them in the portmanteau.

Padlock the trunk. I will let you know later on how you are to send it to me.

Perhaps it will be advisable for you to come here for a few days, to settle a number of matters of importance, which it is impossible to write about. If you agree, we will discuss it in our next letters.

I must close; the post is going. I seem to have forgotten a great many things. Dearest, I know that you have been full of courage and dignity in these terrible days. Go on as you have begun. You win the respect of all. Let me know about Victor's and Adèle's health. As for Charles, he is made of iron.

Give them all my best love, and press the generous hands of Auguste and of Paul Meurice.

My fondest love to you. Do not forget the visit to the M——'s.

VI.

To MME. VICTOR HUGO.

BRUSSELS, *Sunday morning,* 28*th December,* [1851].

Dumas is going to Paris, and undertakes to deliver this letter to you. Dearest, I hope that you are all well there. I shall, perhaps, find some of your letters at the post to-day, and it will be a great joy to me in my solitude. There is nothing new here. Yesterday morning, however, I had a visit from two gendarmes. They laid their hands on me a little; very civilly though. They just conducted me to the *procureur du roi*. They went so far as to march me to the police, to give an explanation of *my forged passport*. The whole thing ended by quasi apologies on their part, by a laugh from me, and good-evening. The Opposition papers here wanted to make a fuss about it. I thought this unnecessary. At heart this government is afraid of the man of the *coup d'état,* and we must not find fault with it for worrying the refugees a little. I forgive them, but the proceedings are none the less very Belgian, — very *welche,* as Voltaire says.

Perhaps it will be feasible to make some arrangement here by which the Belgian booksellers would agree not to pirate the book. It is a great idea. Overtures have been made to me. We shall see what will come of it.

I am working hard at those notes.[1] What a pity that it cannot be published in that form! Well, we shall see what can be done in that direction, too.

Love me, all of you, — Charles, Victor, Auguste, Paul Meurice, my four sons, as I call them. I hope that all these dear prisoners are well. Tell my beloved Adèle to write me a nice little letter, as she did the other day.

Dumas urges me to close my letter. I embrace you all, and I look forward to the day when I shall no longer do it on paper.

VII.

To Mme. Victor Hugo.

Brussels, *Tuesday, 30th December,* [1851].

First and foremost, dearest, do not be uneasy. Mme. Faillet brought me your letter this morning to my inn; but Dumas must have delivered you mine yesterday. By this time you must know what has taken place. A slight annoyance, nothing more, and at the present moment I believe it is completely at an end. Moreover, everybody here shows me the warmest sympathy. It

---

[1] The history of the 2d of December, which Victor Hugo had decided to write on his arrival.

comes from all sides and all parties at once. This morning, when I was lunching at the table I have spoken of, M. de Perseval, the leader of the democratic opposition in the Belgian Chamber, and M. Deschamps, the leader of the Catholic opposition, were sitting near me. Both of them made me a cordial offer of their services. M. Deschamps, who has been minister twice, spoke to me about that little passport affair, and told me that he would intervene in case of need; but that I might consider myself as defended by every one here. He said to me: "There are many who hate you, but everybody honors you."

I believe, in fact, that for the moment I can remain here in perfect safety. In any event, set your mind at rest: England is only a step from here.

Yes, we must consider about the furniture. But, while taking precautions, we must not give way to panic. *They will think twice* before they confiscate my furniture, my rights as an author, and my allowance from the Institute. That would do them more harm than me. So calm yourself, dearest, while keeping a good lookout, however.

I am more popular here than I thought. Yesterday, at a printers' dinner, they drank the health of the three men who personify the struggle against despotism,— Mazzini, Kossuth, Victor Hugo.

I have only space for a couple of lines more. Fondest love to you all. Charlie, Victor, Adèle, I kiss you on your six cheeks. Write to me.

VIII.

To Mme. Victor Hugo.

Brussels, 31*st December,* [1851].

Dearest, — M. Bourlon, who will give you this letter, is the editor of the *Moniteur*, of Belgium. Give him your warmest reception. He is a very distinguished man, with a mind above the common, and a noble heart. He is at one with all our ideas; and his wife, who is witty and charming, also resembles you in enthusiasm and belief in the future and progress.

I send you an article of the *Messager des Chambres* here on the incident which had alarmed you. This will set your mind quite at rest. In spite of this little matter, I am perfectly satisfied with the reception given to me here.

To-day the year closes on a great ordeal for us all, — our two sons in prison and me in exile. That is hard, but good. A little frost improves the crop. As for me, I thank God.

To-morrow, New Year's Day, I shall not be there to embrace you all, my loved ones. But I shall think of you. All my feelings will go out towards you. I shall be in Paris, in the Conciergerie. Talk about me at this family and prison dinner, which I am so sorry to miss; I fancy I shall hear you.

Thank you for the journal which you are keeping for me. I believe it will be very useful, for you see a side of things which escapes me.

Thank Béranger, and send my compliments to Berryer. I shall be delighted to read what Béranger said.

Here I have abundance of information. I am almost

as much surrounded as in Paris. This morning I had a gathering of old representatives and ex-ministers in my den of the Porte-Verte, where I still am.

A *confidential* letter from Louis Blanc has been brought me. They are going to start a weekly paper in London in French. The committee will consist of three Frenchmen, three Germans, and three Italians. I am to be one of the three Frenchmen, with Louis Blanc and Pierre Leroux. What do you say to that? We might make a great fight against the Bonaparte. But I am afraid that it will recoil on our poor dear prisoners. Let me know your views on this point. But be very careful in speaking about it to anybody. *Secrecy is demanded of me.*

Schoelcher arrived this evening, disguised as a priest. I have not seen him yet. The other night I was asleep, and was awakened. It was de Flotte, coming into my room with an advocate from Ghent. He had shaved off his beard. I did not know him. I like de Flotte very much. He is a worthy fellow and a thinker. We talked together for part of the night. Like me, he is full of courage and faith in God.

I embrace you tenderly, my poor dear wife and my beloved children. My fondest love to you. Good-by for the present, Charles. Dearest, give Auguste and Paul Meurice a warm shake of the hand. Give my respects to Mme. Paul Meurice. What a happy time you must all still have together in that prison! How I should like to be with you and with them!

IX.

To Mme. Victor Hugo.

Brussels, *5th January*, 1852.

I have received all the letters of my dear children, and all yours; and the longer they are, the more they please me. So don't be afraid of writing volumes.

You can in case of need, and for non-confidential matters, write to me direct to M. Lanvin, 16 Place de l'Hôtel de Ville. I have taken up my abode there to-day, and have told my landlord that if any one asks for M. Lanvin or for M. Victor Hugo, he is inquiring for me. So I am living there in my two characters.

When Charles arrives he will find me in this vast hall, with three windows looking on the splendid square of the Hôtel de Ville. I have hired (for a mere trifle) the indispensable furniture, a bed, a table, etc., and a good stove. I work there in comfort and feel at home there. If I come across an old carpet for fifteen francs, I shall be perfectly happy.

If I were to send you all the loving things that I have in my heart, it is I who would write you volumes. How can you imagine that I have any mistrust, I who feel that you are such a noble, steadfast, and loving support to me! Withdraw that ugly word. I take precautions, that is all, and I take them in the interest of you all.

You see and feel yourself that my prudence was not carried too far, and that it was justified by the result. Let my sons bear in mind this axiom of my life: it is prudence which gives the right to be courageous.

I send you the letter which Louis Blanc has written

me. Read it yourself and give it to the inmates of the Conciergerie to read. You can return it to me by an early opportunity. Louis Blanc is pressing me for an answer, *yes* or *no*. What do you all say? What do Meurice and Auguste think, and Charles and Victor? It might be of use. Besides, it would be some work ready to hand for Charles. It seems that the capital is found in England. But would there not be a disadvantage in confounding me, even in appearance only, with Louis Blanc and Pierre Leroux? That would deprive me of the isolation of my present position, would connect me with the past of other people, and consequently involve my future in complications which are foreign to me; it would rob me of some of the purity which I now possess, having never had a hand in anything, never been in power, never put forward theories nor made mistakes, but simply held the standard when it was raised, and risked my life on the day of battle.

All is going on well here. Some of the refugees are in low spirits (among them Schoelcher, who, however, behaved in a heroic way), but I cheer them up. This morning there were some lines about me by a student in the *Sancho* (the *Charivari* of Brussels). I decline invitations to dinner and little ovations in family circles. I require my time for work. I have never felt more light-hearted or more pleased with myself. The events in Paris suit me. They reach an ideal point, in atrocity as well as grotesqueness. There are creatures like Troplong, like Dupin, whom I cannot help admiring. I like complete men. These wretches are perfect specimens. They attain the climax of infamy.

I admire this. Bonaparte is well surrounded. I hear that on the sous his eagle will have its head under its wing; good. As for the 7,500,000 votes, even if there were more noughts, I should despise all this rubbish.

My dear, good, brave souls, you are my joy; I embrace you.

X.

To ANDRÉ VAN HASSELT.[1]

BRUSSELS, *6th January*, 1852.

It is not I who am banished, dear sir, but liberty; it is not I whom am exiled, but France. France an outcast from truth, from justice, from greatness, is France in exile and a stranger to herself. Let us pity her and love her more than ever.

I do not suffer. I look and wait. I have fought, I have done my duty; I am vanquished, but happy. A conscience at rest is like a clear sky within one's self.

Soon I shall have my family with me, and I shall wait quietly for God to restore me my country. But I will only have her free.

Ex imo corde.

XI.

To MME. VICTOR HUGO.

BRUSSELS, *Thursday, 8th January*, [1852].

I write to you from my room on the Grande Place, with bright sunshine and the grand Hôtel de Ville before me. Yesterday I inspected the interior of the Hôtel de Ville with the Burgomaster of Brussels, M. de Brouckère, who is most courteously showing me over the town. I continue to be the object of a number of

---

[1] A Belgian writer and poet.

attentions here. The Maupas of Brussels, a certain Baron Hody, who sent me the gendarmes last month, has just been obliged to resign. My affair had something to do with his discomfiture.

We are told here that Xavier Duvieu, Rivière the advocate, and Hippolyte Magen the bookseller, have been transported to Cayenne. This morning I had a visit from the ex-*constituant* Laussedat, whose property has been attached. Horrors are still going on in France. As for Belgium, do not be the least uneasy. The Ministers and the Burgomaster are profuse in cordial assurances. So do not be afraid. I am a sort of centre here. My hall — for my room is a hall — is never empty. Sometimes there are thirty people in it, and I have only two chairs! I shall, however, make an effort to exclude visitors; for if I let in a crowd of intruders, my time will be taken up, and I need it more than ever. I am working hard at my book on the 2d of December. The Belgian papers call Bonaparte *Napoléon le Petit*. So I shall have given names to the two phases of the reactionary movement, *Les Burgraves* and *Napoléon le Petit*. This is an achievement at all events, — in default of something better.

I embrace you, my good and noble wife. Your letters inspire me with faith and strength. Tell my dear little daughter and all the dear children in the Conciergerie to write to me.

I am still expecting Charles at the end of the month. Be careful of what you say.

XII.

To MME. VICTOR HUGO.

BRUSSELS, *Sunday,* 11*th January,* [1852].

You know by this time that I am banished by the Bonaparte, that is to say, *expelled,* this is the word which the fellow uses. Yesterday I was at Schoelcher's; Charras arrived, and we all three had a talk. Charras was telling us about his arrest, his imprisonment, his release, and things of the other world, when Labrousse dropped in and said to me: "You are banished, with sixty-eight representatives of the people, as socialist leaders. . . . I have seen the decree. Your name caught my eye and I was looking for you to tell you of it." "I hope that my name is in the list, too," said Charras. "And mine as well!" said Schoelcher. Whereupon we continued our conversation.

This, however, ought to reassure you a little as regards Belgium. He cannot decently arrest us immediately after the date of our *expulsion.* I am well aware that he does not care a fig for decency. But all the same he will not put forth his hand beyond the frontier to seize us just now. A few months hence, I dare say. But he has plenty to do at the present moment. So set your mind at rest.

I am living, as you know, in the Grande Place. The Burgomaster of Brussels came to see me. I said to him: "Do you know that people say in Paris that the Bonaparte will have me arrested here and carried off at night in my lodging by police agents?" M. de Brouckère (the Burgomaster) shrugged his shoulders and replied: "All you will have to do is to break a pane of glass and call for help. The Hôtel de Ville is close by. There are three sentinels. You will be well defended, never fear!"

I am working hard at the narrative of the 2d of December. Every day materials reach me. The facts which I have are incredible. <u>It will be history, and will read like a romance.</u> Evidently the book will be devoured in Europe. When shall I be able to publish it? At present I do not know.

I have so much to do that I cannot write as many letters to you all as I should like. I should spend my life in writing to you! I seem to be talking to you, my beloved ones. My pen travels at random. The writing is illegible, but what does that matter!

A subscription is being got up here, among us exiles, for the poorest of us. I asked Schoelcher if there was a *maximum*. He said fifteen francs, and I gave him that sum.

Dearest, I fill up the space left with fond love to you all. Write to me, all of you, and *at length*.

XIII.

To PAUL MEURICE.

BRUSSELS, *Sunday*, 11*th January*, 1852.

MY DEAR FRIEND, — My wife has already told you how pleased I was with your letter, and how much I was indebted to you for the details about the 2d of December. Go on sending me everything that you can collect. I am writing a formidable and curious book, which will begin with the facts and end with ideas.

Never was there a finer opportunity or a more inexhaustible subject. I shall treat the Bonaparte in proper fashion. I will see to the fellow's historical future. I will hand him down to posterity by the ears.

Give my respects to your noble wife, and accept a warm shake of the hand for yourself.

XIV.

To the Members of the French Academy.

BRUSSELS, 15*th January*, 1852.

MY DEAR COLLEAGUES, — The political malefactor, whose government lies heavy on France at this moment, has thought fit to issue a decree of expulsion in which he has included me.

My crime is as follows: —

I have done my duty.

I have, by every available means, including armed resistance, defended the Constitution proceeding from universal suffrage, the Republic, and the law against the treachery of the 2d of December.

Those who are banished are forbidden, by order of the *coup d'état*, to reënter France on pain of transportation to Cayenne, that is to say, on pain of death.

In this state of affairs, in face of the brute force which is triumphant, and against which I renew my indignant protests from my place of exile, I am unable to take part in the election to the Academy which will be held on the 22d of January, and I beg you, my dear colleagues, to accept, with the expression of my regret, the assurance of my heartfelt cordiality and my high consideration.

VICTOR HUGO,
Representative of the People.

XV.

To André van Hasselt.

16th January, 1852.

You overwhelm me, my dear colleague; more than that, you stock me with furniture. You send me a sofa to Brussels, — me who cannot even give you a seat in the Academy in Paris. I regret it for our sake, for the luckless Forty. The French Academy would be a little less *welche* if it were to elect a few Belgians like you.

All we can do now is to pity her: the poor Academy looks quite foolish over there. Three exiles! She has not had such a time since 1815. Then it was Louis XVIII. who expelled the other Napoleon, the Great, from the Academy of Sciences.

As for me, I recline luxuriously on your excellent sofa and read your admirable books. O ingratitude of man! I begin to look with scorn on my portmanteau, which I had raised to the dignity of sofa, and which you have deprived of its employment. It is all up, I am transformed from a Spartan into a sybarite. I shall soon come and pay my respects to Mme. van Hasselt and shake you by the hand.

XVI.

To Mme. Victor Hugo.

Brussels, *Saturday,* 17*th January,* [1852].

I have only a minute, dearest wife. I send this by Schoelcher's servant, an old woman who has the courage of ten men, and who has proved it. She will tell you her history. Everything is going on fairly well here. All the Liberal press is on our side, and warmly. I send you some extracts from it about my banishment. A number of papers throughout Belgium have reprinted my speech of 47 on the return of the Bonapartes. It produces a great effect here. I am glad to think that Charles is coming, and that I shall see him in a fortnight. I am convinced that he will prove himself a man here.

I shall probably manage to build a literary citadel, from which we shall bombard the Bonaparte. If not at Brussels, then at Jersey. Hetzel has been to see me. He has a plan similar to mine. Again, Belgium will turn towards us, I think, to protect its bookselling trade. I send you two pages of a pamphlet. Read it, and give it to the inmates of the Conciergerie to read. It is a symptom. Hetzel told me yesterday that a book with the title, *Le Deux Décembre, par Victor Hugo*, would command a sale of at least 200,000 copies.

When we are all four free, we may do some work together. *L'Evénement*, why not? A political propaganda at London, a literary one at Brussels, that is my plan; two centres, and our flame feeding them both.

To bring the matter to a successful issue, I must live like a Stoic and a poor man, and say to them all: I have no need of money; I can wait, you see. A man in want of money is at the mercy of speculators, and is lost. Look at Dumas. I have a pallet, a table, and a couple of chairs. I work all day, and I live at the rate of 1200 francs a year. They feel that I am strong, and I am overwhelmed with offers. When we have settled something, you will join me, and we will make the whole family comfortable again. I want you to be all happy and pleased, — you, my wife, and you, my dear daughter, all of you in fact.

I think that Meurice, Auguste, Charles, and Victor might write a history of the period from February, '48, down to the 2d of December, together.

Distribute the work among yourselves. Each will do his share here. We will work at the same table, with the same inkstand, and the same thoughts. I send you all, in the Tour d'Auvergne and La Conciergerie, the fond love of a happy exile.

I will reply to all of you by the next post. In the mean while write me, all of you, long letters. Dearest, do not forget to fill up the sheets well.

By the way, I have seen the filth which he calls his Constitution!

XVII.

To Mme. Victor Hugo.

Brussels, *Monday, 19th January,* [1852].

This is only a line, which will reach you by the post. Poor Charles will be sad at leaving you; liberty here is not equal to his prison. But it will be a great happiness to me to see him; let this console him. As for Victor, a kiss for him on his two cheeks; and you too, dear little daughter; do not be jealous. But how brave and courageous Victor is! He writes me the calmest, the firmest, the serenest letters imaginable, — with seven months of imprisonment before him! Well done, dear child. You see that I anticipated your thoughts in calling myself "the happy exile" in my last letter.

All kinds of attentions are showered on me here. There is no "people" at present in Belgium; only a bourgeoisie. It *hated* us democrats before it knew us. The Jesuit papers, which abound here, had made bogies of us. Now these worthy men look on us with respect. They are furious at my banishment, which I take quite easily. The other day a city magistrate was reading me the paper in the restaurant. All at once he cried out, *Expulsion!* and gave the table a blow with his fist which broke his jug of beer. Just now I was taking my early cup of chocolate, as usual, at the Café des Mille Colonnes. A young man comes up to me and says: "I am a painter, sir, and I have come to ask a favor of you." "What is it?" "The permission to sketch, from your room, the view of the Grande Place, and to offer you the picture." And he added: "There are only two names in the world, — Kossuth and Victor Hugo."

Similar scenes occur every day. I shall be obliged, on account of this, to breakfast at another café. I attract a crowd there, and that bothers me.

The burgomaster comes to see me occasionally. The other day he said to me: "I am at your disposal. What can I do for you?" "One thing." "What is it?" "Not whitewash the front of your Hôtel de Ville." "But it looks better white." "No, it is better black." "Well, you are an authority. I promise you that the front shall not be whitewashed. But is there anything I can do for yourself?" "One thing." "What is it?" "Blacken the belfry." (They have restored it, not badly, but it is white.) "Goodness! blacken the belfry! but it looks better white." "No, it is better black." "Very well; I will speak to the town councilors, and it shall be done. I will tell them it is for you."

This note is only a line, by the way. Continue to write me long letters. Alas! when shall we all be together again? Oh, if only a good proscription could drive you all out of France!

Love to my Adèle. Greetings to Auguste and Paul Meurice.

XVIII.

To MME. VICTOR HUGO.

Tuesday, 27th January, [1852].

To-morrow Charles will leave the Conciergerie. Dearest, it will be a great blow to you to lose him and a great joy to me to have him. I want him on his return home to find this letter from me, which will tell him that I am expecting him to come as soon as he can.

This is my mode of life and will be his here: I leave No. 16 at the end of the month, and move to No. 27 in the same Grande Place. There we shall have two bedrooms, one with a fireplace and a south aspect. The latter is large and we can work together in it. I propose to take it myself. If, however, Charles, who feels the cold, would like the room with a fire for getting up in the morning, I will let him have it for the rest of the winter and move into it myself in the spring, if we are still at Brussels. I have taken these rooms at No. 27 from the 1st of February. As for expenditure, it must be most strictly limited, as the future is more than doubtful, and resources which are seemingly safest may fail us altogether or for a time. I live on 100 francs a month. Here is the daily estimate:—

Rent	1 fr. 00
Breakfast (a cup of chocolate)	0 fr. 50
Dinner	1 fr. 25
Firing	0 fr. 25
	3 fr. 00

That makes 90 francs for myself. The balance (10 francs) is for washing, tips, etc. Charles and I will therefore spend 200 francs a month between us. In this way we shall go on working until some arrangement is made here or in London. Once a market for our writings is assured, we shall be able to add to our own and the general comfort. In seven months, dearest, you will all join us. By that time the situation will have become clearer. We shall have settled something. I shall have sold all or part of my manuscripts or my reprints, and we shall all be able to found, somewhere or other, in some beautiful and safe spot, a happy colony.

Talking of that, Brofferio has written me a charming letter asking me to come to Piedmont and offering me a villa on the Lago Maggiore. So cheer up. And when I speak of *all*, of course I mean my *four sons*. Meurice and Auguste belong to the family.

I write this in haste, dearest. To-morrow, or the day after at latest, Mme. K., who is spending a few days here, will bring you another letter, and letters for Auguste, for Paul Meurice, for my Victor, for my darling daughter, and for Charles, if he has not arrived here. Let me know the day and hour of his arrival.

Send me my portfolio and my albums of sketches by Charles. Before sending them, let Paul Meurice, Auguste, and Mme. Bouclier each choose a sketch from the albums.

Dearest mamma, in a couple of days you will get a longer letter. I think it is best to sublet, and I will explain to you what I consider feasible. In the mean while continue to be *radiant*. Mélanie's remark is stupid and worthy of her. Yes, *be radiant*. We are passing through a useful and splendid period of adversity. Everything that is happening is of use, to France as a lesson, to our children as an ordeal, to us both as a bond of love and a hallowing of our life.

I approve beforehand of all that you do and all that you say. I know that you have a wise mind and a great heart. You could not have given Villemain a better answer. He is a friend, however, and I will write to him.

One more word for you all. I love you dearly.

XIX.

To Mme. Victor Hugo.

Brussels, *Wednesday, 28th January,* [1852].

I begin, dearest, by thanking you for everything. This letter will be brought to you by Madame de Kisseleff. I spent a most pleasant evening at her house yesterday. She invited me to meet Girardin, whom, in fact, I had not seen. We had called on each other without meeting. Girardin said to me: "Finish your book quickly, if you want it to appear before the end of this régime." I found him, however, in certain respects, skeptical and Bonapartist. He said to me: "Mme. de Girardin is as red as you are. She is furious, and she talks of 'the bandit' like you." He believes that the

Bonaparte will fall in three months, unless he goes to war, — which Persigny will urge him to do. In that case Belgium, he said, would be invaded at the end of March. It would be necessary to seek a place of safety before that.

There has been a *re*disposition to expel me from here. The Belgian ministry stood its ground, and was shaken by it. Read what I write to Victor on this subject. By the way, you must all read all the letters which I address to each. It is the same letter that I continue, and, as I suppose that you all read it, I do not repeat facts. It is also necessary to be very prudent at the Conciergerie. Read my letters, and speak of them only among yourselves. Be on your guard against the police, — *always at hand and on the lookout.* You must be more watched now than ever.

All that you tell me of the effect of the spoliation decree is wonderfully true and just. That epitome of every crime, the Second of December, has produced less impression on the bourgeois, whether shopkeeper or banker, than this confiscation.[1] To meddle with the law is a trifle; to lay hands on a family is everything. The poor bourgeoisie has its heart in its breeches' pocket. It is improving a little, however, they say, and the Liberal opposition is reappearing. This is a good sign; and what I admire is the courage of the women. Everywhere the women are raising their heads before the men. I applaud them with all my heart.

Now let us talk of Charles. He is coming here. He must work, or die of ennui and vacuity. But at what? There are no *paying* papers, and besides the

[1] The confiscation of the property of the Orléans family.

Belgian government would not allow a French writer to make use of the liberty of the press here. What is to be done? What useful work is there for him? Here is what has occurred to me: in the first place, what I have already written to Charles, the four to write a history of the last four years with the help of the *Evénement* collection, and distribute the work among themselves before Charles leaves; Charles would do his share here, and the book would sell very well, *in a finished state;* this is the way things are managed in Belgium.

Secondly, why should Charles not see Houssaye and Gautier before he starts? He might send them from here *non-political* letters on Belgium for the *Revue de Paris*, which he would do admirably. It seems to me that he might make a hundred francs or so a month in this way. I would keep him, and that would give him pocket-money.

Think this over; hold a consultation in the great council of the Conciergerie. Let Charles take the advice of our two dear burgraves, Auguste Vacquerie and Paul Meurice.

Thank Béranger for me. As for Villemain, I am grateful to him for everything. I am grateful to him for having made the offer to you, and to you for having refused it. Dearest, I am delighted to find you so completely at one with me.

I send you all my heart, my thought, my life. I send you, you specially, my fondest love.

XX.

To ANGELO BROFFERIO.

BRUSSELS, 2d *February*, 1852.

My eloquent and dear Colleague, — I thank you from the bottom of my heart. As orator, you answered me from your tribune; as exile, you bid me welcome.

I was glad of your sympathy as a politician and a citizen; I am proud of the offer of hospitality which you make me with such dignity, which I should accept with such pleasure.

I do not know what Providence has in store for me; imperious public duties have a greater call on me than ever. It may be necessary for me not to leave the frontier nearest to Paris. Brussels and London are posts of combat. The writer must now take the place of the speaker; I shall continue with the pen the war which I waged against despots with my voice. It is the Bonaparte, the Bonaparte alone, whom I must now grapple with; to do this I may have to remain here or go to London. But depend on it that the day when I can leave Belgium or England, it will be for Turin. I shall be delighted to grasp you by the hand. What a number of things you combine in yourself! You are Italy, that is to say, glory; you are Piedmont, that is to say, liberty; you are Brofferio, that is to say, eloquence. Yes, I certainly shall go and see you before long, and see your villa on the Lago Maggiore; I shall visit you, to find all that I love, blue sky, sunshine, untrammeled thought, fraternal hospitality, nature, poetry, friendship. When my second son has come out of prison, I shall be able to realize this dream and gather my family around your fireside.

We shall speak of France, now, alas! resembling Italy, fallen and great; we shall speak of the inevitable future, of the assured triumph, of the last necessary war, of the great federal Continental parliament, in which I shall perhaps have the supreme joy of sitting by your side.

XXI.
To MME. VICTOR HUGO.

Saturday, 14th February, [1852].

Do not say, dearest, that I have no time to read. Write me nice long letters, I beg of you. Do not get out of the sweet habit of having long talks with me on paper. Your letter, which is so short, reached us yesterday evening, Friday. We had not had any for ten days after Charles's arrival. I have very little time for writing. I get up at eight (I wake up Charles, who generally stays in bed in spite of this), and then I set to work. I go on working up to twelve; then comes breakfast. Up to three I have visitors. At three, I begin work again. At five, dinner. Digestion (a stroll or a visit) up to ten o'clock. At ten I come home and work till twelve. At twelve I make my bed and retire to rest. I make my bed for the following reason: the sheets are about the size of napkins and the blankets no bigger than table-covers. I have been obliged to invent a plan of arranging them so as to have my feet covered, and every night I make my bed. Charles sleeps through it all.

I promised our dear Paul Meurice a drawing. The one out of the small album does not count. By the side of my bed, in front of the looking-glass, behind the lacquered box with a small lid, there is a large well-executed sketch representing two castles, of which one is in the distance. Have a white margin of about three inches put round it, and give it to Paul Meurice from me. Thank him for his charming letter. Tell Auguste, — who writes to me, as he always does, a letter full of profound observations, — tell Meurice and Victor, that I will write them the lines they want. The least I can do for them is to send them a few stanzas in their imprisonment.

Charles is very kind and nice. He makes up to me a little for the separation from you all. The difficult thing is to make him work. Up to the present I have only been able to get out of him a few pages, — very well done, however, — on what took place in the Conciergerie. Tell our three prisoners to put down their reminiscences and those of the others, and to send me all the facts that they can.

I return to Charles. Pending *L'histoire des quatre années*, which Hetzel thinks an excellent thing and likely to sell well, I told him to write a book on his six months' imprisonment and our journey to Lille. *La Conciergerie et les Caves* would be a good, interesting volume. He promises to do it, he is as gentle as a lamb, but he does not begin. I do not complain, for I don't want you to scold him. I work enough for all. Only I am afraid that time will be wasted. The years fly by and habits are formed.

The other night he had gone out and I was at work. At twelve o'clock a knock at the door. "Come in." "Monsieur," says the landlady, "has your son a key?" (of the street door). "No, he has not." "Then I will wait up for him." "No, don't do that." "What then?" "You go to bed. I will come down into your shop [the entrance is a tobacco shop]; I can write just as well at your counter as at my table, and I will sit up for him."

I went down to the counter, perched myself on the shopwoman's high stool, and wrote there. At three in the morning Charles came in, and was astounded to find me scribbling at the counter and sitting up for him. I did not reproach him, but since then he has never come in later than twelve.

As regards my negotiations with the booksellers, people in Belgium are afraid, and a free book-trade in this country, even for purely literary works, is impossible at the present moment. The success which I thought within my grasp eludes me. So we must wait for a time. Hetzel is going to London and will try to get it done there. All this makes it necessary for us to adhere strictly to our economical life of exiles, living on three francs a day. However, I give Charles a little pocket-money occasionally. It all goes in smoke.

Just now there was a knock at my door. I left off my letter. It was the manager of the *Variétés*, M. Carpier, who had come from Paris, he said, on purpose to see me. He asked me, with many entreaties and offers, to write a play for Frédéric, *Don César*. He said a great deal about Auguste, whose eminent success as a dramatist he foresees. He seemed to me an intelligent man. He told me that Maupas had uttered a cry of delight at the idea of a play from me, fancying, no doubt, that literature would take me away from politics. I told him that I would see about it after the publication of my book, but that I could only break silence now by a slap in the face to the *coup d'état*. He offered to bring his company to rehearse at Brussels or in London, wherever I might be. I am to see him again.

Farewell for the present, dear, dearest wife. My love to Dédé, and a great deal to yourself.

XXII.
To Mme. Victor Hugo.

Brussels, 22*d February*, [1852].

I begin by telling you that you are a noble and admirable woman. Your letters bring tears to my eyes. Everything is in them, — dignity, strength, simplicity, courage, reason, serenity, tenderness. When you discuss politics you do it well, your judgment is good and your remarks to the point. When you discuss business and family matters, you show your large, kind heart. How, then, can you imagine that I have a shadow of an *arrière-pensée* with you, or with any one? What have I to hide from you, — from you above all people?

My life will bear the closest scrutiny and so will my inmost thoughts. You do not like to speak to me about money matters. I can quite understand it. We are poor, and we must try to pass with credit through an ordeal which may come to an end soon, but which may last long. I wear out my old shoes and my old clothes; that is easy enough. You have to bear privations, pain, penury even; that is not so easy because you are a wife and mother, but you do it gladly and nobly. How, then, could I mistrust you? About what and for what reason? Is not everything which I have yours? Do not say *your* money, say *our* money. I am the administrator, that is all. As soon as I see my poor sons working as I do, as soon as I find a market and a publisher somewhere, at Brussels or in London, no matter where, provided it is in a free country, as soon as I have sold a manuscript, then I will hold my hand and make the whole family more comfortable. In the mean while, we must suffer a little. As for me, it is your sufferings which pain me and not my own.

All this accounts for my strictness in the matter of expenditure. Our income is not yet assured, and at present does not cover our expenses. That will come, but is not the case yet. How can you see any distrust in that? It is merely cautiousness, such as I have with regard to myself. You know well that all my life through I have begun privations and economies with myself. Dearest, I am ready to make over our whole fortune to you; can you doubt it? I would only say to you: Be careful. One fine day I may fail you, and we must try to have the capital intact after I am gone.

The dignity of your character even requires it. I want you always to be independent of everybody. Live as you have always lived, whether with me or without me, proudly, worthily, looking down upon governments, men, and things, and not caring for or needing protection. That is the future which I should like for you and for the children. This is the reason, I repeat it, of my present strictness.

I see from the answer which Charles gives you and which he has shown me that you scolded him a little in your letter. Do not scold him. I want to see him pleased and happy by my side, and if he will not work, how can we help it? Some day or other, I hope, reason will come, something will tempt him, and he will set to work. In the mean while I try to make him happy. I do not reproach him, I give him complete liberty, and I do what I can to make him like living with me. I am sorry that he does not tell you anything of this in his letter. Some day my children will know all that I have been to them.

My book is getting on. I could finish it in a week (working at night), if necessary. But I do not see any need for hurry. Every day I receive fresh information which obliges me to write parts of it over again. This is a great nuisance. I am not afraid of work, but I dislike work that is thrown away. I am not sure whether I shall add the events in the provinces to those in Paris. That might make it long and monotonous. Besides, Paris alone decides everything, and entirely decided the Second of December, as usual. Probably I shall only give a summary of the most interesting events in the provinces, just enough to show up the fiction of the alleged excesses. And then I think it is better, both for the propaganda and for the sale, that the book should be in one volume.

As regards the paper,[1] as at present advised, I agree with Auguste. Nothing can be done under this law. If a literary paper could be made a success, we might think about it, however. Politics would be confined to facts, and a splendid literary opposition would be

[1] A proposal had been made to republish the *Evénement* in a literary form.

started. But would this be permitted? Consult among yourselves. You are nearer the scene of action.

Talking of good politics and good literature, here is a noble letter: —

MONSIEUR, — As I do not admit your right to plunder my family, I cannot admit your right to assign me an allowance in the name of France. I refuse the dowry.   HÉLÈNE D'ORLÉANS.

Charles will tell you that I took him to Louvain. I had a great reception there. The librarian was waiting for me at the library, the director of the Academy at the Academy, the city magistrate at the Hôtel de Ville. I was presented with a medal. The curé was not waiting for me at the church. I went there, however. The town was all agog. The students of the University followed me in the streets at a distance. One of them wrote to me as follows: "We did not cheer you for fear of offending our poor little government."

Dearest, I am finishing this at ten o'clock at night. I am going to send it to Serrière, who starts to-morrow morning. Several representatives — Yvan, Labrousse, Barthélemy — are with me who are talking of you, and who send you their respects. I will write to Abel and to Béranger. I will write to my Victor and my brave and charming little Adèle. I say "little," although she is as big as you, but I still see her a tiny little thing, and saying, *Papa é i.*

Thank Meurice for his kind and interesting letter, and embrace all my inmates of the Conciergerie. Love to you, to you all.

XXIII.

To MME. VICTOR HUGO.

25th February, [1852].

I have spent the day with Marc Dufraisse, he dictating to me, and I writing. In this way I have scribbled twenty closely written pages without realizing it, the result of which is, dearest, that I am worn out this evening. I wanted to write to all my Conciergerie, I wanted to write to my darling Adèle, and I have hardly time to send you a dozen lines. The big packet must be for next time.

Yesterday I invited Girardin to dinner, and we talked together very cordially. He told me of an article of Gautier's which touches me. Thank Gautier for me. Girardin said that it was charming, and promised to send it me, as well as one by Janin. So you must thank Janin, too. I am sure that thanks coming from you will please him still more than if they came from me. I have just read a good paragraph in the *Emancipation*, a Jesuit and Bonapartist paper here. I transcribe it for you. The subject is the *Corps Législatif:* —

> The elections are perfectly free. Yet a paper which should venture to suggest the name of Victor Hugo or of Charras to the electors would inevitably be suspended.

This is delightful. Here is what the *Messager des Chambres* says on the same subject: —

> What the ministry of the interior concedes ostensibly, freedom of voting, the police has orders to withdraw. Thus in the Faubourg Saint-Antoine several workmen, heads of families, have been threat-

ened with a prosecution for clandestine printing, — for having printed, with one of the small lithographic presses which every tradesman possesses, tickets with the name of Victor Hugo.

Of all the exiles, the illustrious poet is the one for whom M. Bonaparte has the most hatred: it is personal animosity, enhanced by the constantly increasing popularity of the poet. Detested in aristocratic and middle-class circles before the *coup d'état*, M. Hugo has regained all the ground lost in them. He is now considered one of the most energetic champions of law and liberty.

Shrove Tuesday here is very frolicsome, and rather farcical. From my room on the Grande Place I could see the centre of the masquerades. My window was a box for the play. The Flemings have a sleepy look all the year through. On Shrove Tuesday there comes an access of gayety which makes them wild. They are very funny in this state. They get five at a time into the same blouse, with enormous hats on, and dance together. They smear their faces, cover themselves with flour, paint themselves black, red, and yellow; it is killing. Yesterday the Grande Place was full of scenes from Teniers and Callots. And then deafening blasts from trumpets all the night. Under my window I read the following notice: *Société des Crocodiles. Dernier grand bal.*

My book is getting on. I am pleased with it. I read some friends a few pages, which produced a great effect. I believe that it will be a signal victory of intelligence over brute force, — inkstand against cannon. The inkstand will smash the cannon.

I feel that I am liked by everybody here. The burgomaster and the town councilors are most attentive. I believe that I rule the town a little. Really, all these Belgians are very nice. They say that they hate the

French. At heart they have a great respect for them. *I* am quite fond of the worthy Belgians.

My darling daughter, play my air *Brama* from time to time, and think of me while doing so. Tell your dear mother to write me a long letter, and set her the example. My Victor, do you do the same. Send me plenty of big sheets from everybody, beginning with yourself. I long to read your letters, and to embrace you all.

Love to Auguste and Meurice. Have you given Meurice the large sketch with the two castles?

XXIV.

To MME. VICTOR HUGO.

Friday, 27th February, [1852].

M. Coste, of the *Evénement*, will take you this note. Dearest, he is fortunate: he will see you and all the others.

I have been rather unwell lately. Always at work, going out very little, hardly taking any exercise, I who used to be such a great walker; this made me feel out of sorts. I was feverish for a few days, but it is gone now.

Charles and I still get on nicely and quietly together. If he would only set to work seriously and of his own accord, I should be almost happy here, if the word "happy" can be used when you are not here, my beloved, noble wife; when you are not here, my dear children; when you are absent, you who are the joy of my life!

We live with our eyes turned toward Paris, awaiting your letters, dearest; awaiting a big packet from the

Conciergerie. It is raining; the weather is cold; it is Lent; we feel lonely. We sadly want a ray of sunshine. It depends on you to send it us.

Tell Victor, tell Auguste, tell M. and Mme. Paul Meurice that Charles and I are constantly talking of them. Yesterday, at the exiles' table, Charles recited some lines of Auguste's which set the whole colony in a roar. It was the story of *Madame Revel* replaced by *Philippe-le-Bel.* You probably know it.

Embrace them all for me, — even the men, and especially the women.

This is only a line to bid you good-morning, — a small interruption in my work. Give my Victor-Toto and my Adèle-Dédé two kisses for me.

XXV.
To THE SAME.

BRUSSELS, 17*th March*, [1852].

Charles was getting into idle ways, and wasting his time. On the other hand, he said he wanted gloves, cabs, pocket-money, etc. I have made an arrangement with him. I am to give him fifty francs a month for his personal expenses, and he is to get up in the morning at eight, as I do, and work in my room until eleven. On the strength of these three hours I am to let him off work for the rest of the day. He accepted with enthusiasm; he got up and worked the first and the second day; but he is falling off already. Yesterday he worked for half an hour, and to-day not at all. I scolded him a little. At first he protested, in his usual way; then he understood, and I hope that from tomorrow he will be regular. These fifty francs a month will inconvenience me, but I had rather he did not get into debt, and that he worked a little. You approve what I have done, I hope? Oh, how I wish I had you with me, and how I want you here to keep him up to the mark! Do not scold him for it, however. Perhaps he will really set to work now. Behave as if I had told you nothing about it.

His tastes lie in the direction of small plays, light poetry, of facile and sterile things. I try to check this, and to direct his mind towards serious work, calculated to promote his views and be of service to him in the future. I insist on his writing his book on the Conciergerie. Do you speak to him about it, too.

As for me, you can picture my life. It is still the same. I get up at eight; work; breakfast at eleven, — we have got beyond chocolate, Charles preferred a cutlet; visitors up to three; work till five; table d'hôte dinner, with Charles, Dumas, Noël Parfait, Bancel, etc., up to ten; from ten to twelve work. I dine out sometimes, but not often. There is a nice rich old Polish lady here, — Mme. de Laska, — who is very fond of Charles. I have dined there once. Last week I met Girardin, Quinet, and Dumas, when dining with a publisher here, — M. Muquardt. The Brussels publishers are afraid of my book on the Second of December. I shall evidently be obliged to publish it in London. The important point, however, is to do it. It will certainly be published, — how, or by whom, does not matter.

XXVI.

To Mme. Victor Hugo.

Brussels, 19*th March*, [1852].

Dearest, you will have received through Mme. Noël Parfait a letter for M. Duboy, advocate of the court of appeal. *It is of great importance to get the reply to this letter as soon as possible.* The following will explain.

I want details of what took place at the High Court on the Second of December for my book. Marc Dufraisse has written to M. Duboy, whom he knows, for these details. Try to get a reply from M. Duboy. Send to his house. Perhaps it would not be advisable to tell him that the information is for me. That might be an excuse for not communicating it.

Since I wrote to you, Charles has taken to work again a little. Press him in the same direction as I do: a solid, serious book, with the stamp of exile on it, and making it impossible for any one to say that he has learned nothing from his imprisonment.

He is in great request here. He is very nice, and that accounts for it. I advise him to be dignified and serious, even with women. No levity, no debts, and work before play. He agrees to everything, and I will try to make him practice it. But I sadly need you to help me. Write to him always from this point of view, without ever scolding him.

Yesterday I saw Girardin, and we had a good long talk. He is publishing a socialist book here to-morrow, and starts for Paris the same day. I do not think that all you have heard of him is true. I found him very satisfactory yesterday; I said to him: "Go to Paris as little as possible, remain there as little as possible, be as much of an exile as possible."

He thanked me and made rather an interesting remark. He said to me: "You have been the dart. You flew an immense distance in an incredibly short space of time, and you buried yourself so deep in democracy that no power on earth will be able to pull you out of it."

If you see Mme. de Girardin, congratulate her from me on her courage and her moral grandeur.

Dearest, do not forget that I must have a dozen or so good pages next time. All your letters are full of beauty and strength. If I needed energy, they would give it me. Let us be of good hope. All is well when the head is well, and we have never had a clearer or better idea of our position than now.

Kiss my Victor, kiss my Adèle, and tell them to kiss you. I shall seem to be among you. My love to Paul Meurice and Auguste Vacquerie. My kind regards to Mme. Paul.

XXVII.

To Mme. Victor Hugo.

Brussels, *Monday, 22d March,* [1852].

Good-morning, dear mamma. This is only a hasty line to tell you that we are well and to send you Dumas' article, which is so nice for you. Write and thank him. He will be much touched by it.

M. Carpier, the manager of the *Variétés*, is here again, "to see me," he still says. I repeated the categorical statement which I had already made him, that it was impossible for me to write anything for the theatre, and especially a comedy, before I had performed a political act and published my book. He said: "But after your book has come out they will prohibit your piece." "Very possibly," I rejoined, "but it is my duty." He told me, by the way, that the Elysée was much alarmed about my book, and that Romieu had spoken to him of it with *anxiety*. Good! He wants Charles to write a play for him. Provided Charles writes it in verse, so as to dispel all idea of a light piece, and provided also he has published or finished his *Conciergerie* beforehand, I quite approve, and I urge him to do it.

Hetzel says that a line from me to Desnoyers would open the columns of the *Siècle* to Charles. I will send it you. Charles might send the *Siècle* non-political letters on Brussels. Let me know your views.

I am up to the neck in my cesspool of the Second of December. As soon as I have emptied it, I shall cleanse the wings of my mind and publish some poetry.

XXVIII.
To the Same.

Friday, 26th March, [1852].

Charles will explain, dearest, why our letters are so hurried. However, if my letters are short, they are frequent, and besides, you know how I work. Really, you owe me a page for every line of mine.

I should like to be able to write to you at length, for I have a piece of news to tell you. A few days ago, I received a visit from an Imperialist, an old friend of mine, and a friend of Louis Bonaparte. He was on his way through Brussels, he said, and did not like to leave without shaking me by the hand. He said that Louis Bonaparte was grieved at the *fatality* which separates us.

"It is not fatality," I said, "it is crime. And his crime is a gulf." He resumed: "He is well aware of the obligations under which the family is to you. He hesitated for five days before putting your name on the proscription list." "Ah!" I said with a laugh, "he would have preferred putting me on the roll of the Senate, eh? Well, tell him this, that the roll of the Senate is the proscription list. To be an outcast from France is only a misfortune. To be an outcast from honor is real misery."

The worthy man will be a Senator one of these days. He took his departure.

XXIX.
To Mme. Victor Hugo.

Brussels, 8*th April*, [1852].

More impromptu notes, dearest. Our dear good Deschanel, who will bring you this, is starting for Paris in an hour. Receive him as one of our best friends, as he is. I saw by a few lines from Paul in the *Indépendance* (thank Paul from me) that you had taken steps, and to some purpose, about the silly rumors spread by the Elysée on the subject of my *solicited return*. I had replied at once here by the following: —

Several papers announce that M. Victor Hugo has been *authorized* to return to France. It is difficult to account for such a report. M. Hugo formerly procured for M. Bonaparte permission to return to France. He has no need to solicit it from him to-day.

Now you know all about my dialogue with the Elysée. I hope that this will silence him.

Dearest mamma, I spent such a nice evening yesterday. Alexandre Dumas has arrived, we dined together, and spoke about you. He told me again how every one loves and respects you, and I told him that every one is quite right.

You will have seen Hetzel. He will have spoken to you about my book, and pointed out to you the difficulties in the way of publishing it. These obstacles will disappear. M. Trouvé-Chauvel, the ex-Minister of Finance, came to see me just now. I think he will go to London and see to the publication of my book. There were three ex-Ministers of 1848 in my room, Charras, Freslon, and Trouvé-Chauvel. I read them a few pages of my manuscript. The effect was good. Trouvé-Chauvel said: "The book will be an event and a monument."

Have you seen this story?

> M. Villemain having been obliged to go to the Elysée on some matter relating to the French Academy, M. Bonaparte said to him in rather a sour tone: "Monsieur Villemain, the French Academy won't make friends with me; it is not like the Academy of Sciences, which has given me three Senators." "The French Academy is more fortunate," replied M. Villemain, "it has given you three exiles."

This exhausts my budget of news for to-day. But my heart is full. I could go on writing to you on that subject indefinitely. Charles has gone out, but I send you his fond love as well as mine, and also to Dédé and Toto. I am very weary of Toto's imprisonment. If he is as weary of my exile, it will be a joyful day when we meet again. I have heard of Paul Meurice's great success. Congratulate him and embrace him for me.

My warmest regards to Auguste.

XXX.

To Mme. Victor Hugo.

Brussels, 14*th April*, [1852].

Dearest mamma, I send you a line for Paul Meurice. His success [1] has been a great pleasure to us here. We drank his health; tell him that.

I have twice had a visit which I cannot describe at length, but which I will tell you about on the happy day when we meet again. It was from the physician of the Orléans family, M. Guéneau de Mussy. Although he denied it, it seemed to me that he had a mission. He is a superior man, however, and was very nice in every way. He told me that the Orléans family had never forgotten that I was the last person who proclaimed the Regency on the 24th of February in the Place de la Bastille, when all their friends were concealing themselves and disappearing. He told me that the Duchess of Orléans said of me in a tone of grief: "*What! is it possible that he is not our friend!*"

I spoke to him warmly of the Orléans princes, and in particular with great respect and profound sympathy of the Duchess of Orléans. But I ended by saying: "However, I belong for good and all to the Republic." I think he must have understood.

The weather has been very fine here for some days, but I cannot take advantage of it, working almost all day. At this moment I have splendid sunshine on this

---

[1] The drama *Benvenuto Cellini*.

letter, and my window is wide open. The only thing which tires me is that I am frequently obliged to rewrite parts of my book, owing to the receipt of fresh information. Oh! how well I understand the remark of the abbé Vertot : *Mon siège est fait !*[1]

My affection of the larynx has almost disappeared; a dull, settled pain in the heart has come in its place. They tell me that I ought to take exercise and work less, and this is the very thing I cannot do. I must hope for the best!

We think here that all is going on satisfactorily in Paris. I rather distrust our judgment as exiles, and I try not to flatter myself. After all, let Providence do as it thinks fit. I have ten years of exile at the service of the Republic.

Dearest, nothing can be nobler, more dignified, or better than your letters. Their only fault is that they are sometimes short. So write to me at length and often.

XXXI.

To THE SAME.

BRUSSELS, 19*th April*, [1852].

Dearest, I answer your letter at once. I am very pleased with my Toto. Impress this on him and kiss him for me on both cheeks. Everybody congratulates

---

[1] An allusion to an anecdote well known in France. The abbé Vertot was a writer of the eighteenth century, the historian of the Order of Malta. He had asked a friend for some documents relating to a very important siege sustained by Malta. The documents were a long time in coming, but at last the friend brought them; they were authentic and of great importance. "Too late," cried the abbé Vertot. *"Mon siège est fait !"* (I have finished the history of the siege!) The remark has become proverbial in France.

me warmly about him. People stop me in the street to say: You have a son who is worthy of you. Only he must understand that *dignité oblige.* He must go on as he has begun, and he and Charles must take life seriously. Everything that you write to me on this point is profoundly just and true. Do you hear, Victor? Trust your mother and follow her advice.

So I am going to see you all again, and we shall resume our happy family life. This fills us with joy here. But we must make our plans rapidly and at once.

If I sell my book in England, as seems more and more probable, I shall leave Belgium in a fortnight or three weeks. It would perhaps be unadvisable for you to come and settle here, take an apartment, etc., for such a short time. In that case this is my idea: as soon as my book is sold, I would go to London and from there straight to Jersey. Jersey is a very pretty island belonging to England, seventeen leagues from the coast of France. Living is comfortable and cheap there. All the exiles say that it is very nice. I would try to find, and probably should find, an apartment in Jersey, perhaps a small house, with a sea-view and southern aspect, and — why not? — a garden. We would settle ourselves in Jersey as comfortably as possible, and the Bonaparte might last as long as he liked, it would be all the same to us. We could go to London in the winter and spend the summer in Jersey. French is spoken in Jersey, which is important, as none of us know English.

I may add that our friends would join us. We should have a spare room for Auguste, a floor for M.

and Mme. Paul Meurice, and from there we could work together at the *Moniteur universel des peuples*, of which I am now laying the foundations with M. Trouvé-Chauvel. He starts for London to-morrow, with notes dictated by me. He is enthusiastic about my idea of a triple publication in London, Brussels, and New York, and of a *Journal des peuples* edited by Kossuth, Mazzini, etc., and myself. I think we shall do great things. But all this obliges us to leave Belgium. I am sorry, for it is a nice country and would have been very pleasant in the summer. Just now we are troubled with cold.

Let me know what you think of all this, dearest mamma. If you prefer to come at once, do not hesitate to say so. I shall make no objection, never fear! If you think it advisable to adopt my plan, discuss it with Dédé and Toto, and write to me about it.

In any event, I will do what you wish, what you all wish, my beloved ones.

My pain in the heart is better. Fond love to you and the children. Consult Auguste about my plan. My warmest regards to him and to Meurice.

XXXII.

To MME. VICTOR HUGO.

BRUSSELS, 30*th April*, [1852].

Dearest, the day before yesterday, as Lamoricière was leaving my room, Bixio arrived and gave me your letter.

You scold me for the shortness of my letters, and I thank you for scolding me; but I do not deserve it. I write incessantly; the farther I get, the greater the mass of material. It is now clear that there will be two volumes. In the morning I write the book; after twelve o'clock I get up the case, take down *evidence*, listen to witnesses, etc. In the evening I work at the book again. I have not even time for an hour's walk in the day; barely half an hour, after dinner, — and besides, it is very cold in the evening. You see that when I write, two pages from me is more meritorious than ten from any one else. However, I delight in talking to you.

Charles has set to work, and, I hope, in earnest. He will write and we shall send you before long the first letter to the *Siècle*. It is rather a difficult thing to do. To avoid politics at a time like this and to manage to be interesting is no easy matter. But I am sure that Charles will get through it admirably.

Dearest, if the non-settlement of my affairs in London should entail a longer stay here, we would take steps at once, and you should join us immediately. We are as anxious to have you as you are to have us. Our life here is all broken up, and we long to have a home again, — the only real happiness for exiles.

I have not much space left, and will fill it with affectionate messages. I embrace you and Dédé and Victor. Tell Victor that Charles is working. Now, then, a race between Victor and Charles! I embrace you once more. Our warmest regards to Vacquerie, and to Meurice, whose *Benvenuto* delights me.

XXXIII.

To Mme. Victor Hugo.

Brussels, 12*th May*, 9 p. m., [1852].

Dearest, your letter has reached me. Although I do not reproach myself, for my whole time is spent in unremitting labor, I am sorry to think that you have been a fortnight without letters, and that you are in low spirits. I want you to get two letters, one after another. Charles, who has worked hard all the week, has gone to the theatre this evening to see Mme. Guyon act, and I am staying at home to write to you.

I have not yet seen the man from London. I was expecting him yesterday, and I still expect him. I am afraid, sad to say, that even in England there is no such thing as a free press, and that they shrink from publishing my book. This is between ourselves, for you must not mention this hitch to any one. The people at the Elysée would be delighted to hear of it, and would try to throw more difficulties in the way. In that case my mind is made up: I shall publish the book at my own expense, no matter how.

By this time you will have received Charles's article. It is very remarkable, and will, I think, be much noticed. As soon as the first article is inserted, I am sure that Charles will work, — and that is a great point.

My dear wife, my dear little daughter, my Victor, how I miss you! I am often very sad here. I long for the time when we shall all meet. I should like to see a smile on the sweet face of my Adèle-Dédé. Do you know, my Dédé, that it will soon be six months —

six months — since I saw you! And you, my Victor, make your mother happy till I come.

I take refuge from all my sad thoughts in work, — work in the morning, work in the day, work at night. But all this toil is another source of sadness, an austere task of punishment and of justice.

When we are together, I shall write some verses, I shall publish a big volume of poetry. I shall rejoice in it, and I think we shall have a charming time. Would that it had arrived already!

Mme. Guyon has brought me a very noble letter from Janin. Thank him if you meet him. Tell our dear Théophile, too, how touched I am at reading my name in his fine articles.

XXXIV.

To Mme. Victor Hugo.

Brussels, 30*th May*, [1852].

I answer you without delay, dearest, and you will get this letter to-morrow morning. I send it direct, so as not to lose time. All the plans you have made are excellent. Go on; it is impossible to do better. Dearest, I am distressed to think that you are alone over there, and that you have to provide for so many things all at once. But I too, you know, am hard at work; I do not waste a minute.

Charles had a letter from Victor yesterday. The poor child has some trouble; you will know what it is. He asks me to take him in here. We wrote to him to come directly. I imagine he will arrive on Tuesday morning. We will try to occupy him and console him. But you will be still more lonely. That makes me all the more anxious to hasten the time when we shall all be together, — a happy time, you will see!

. . . .

My beloved, this letter is nothing but business from beginning to end. I have hardly been able to tell you a word of what I feel. I could not do without you, do you understand? You have been great and admirable throughout all these trials. Do not doubt for a moment, either of the present or of the future. You will see what a happy little group we shall be in Jersey. Charles and I send our fondest love to you. If there is any delay about Jersey, you must come and join us at Brussels. Tell Victor that his room (your room) is ready.

Dearest wife and daughter, I love you. You are my delight and my joy.

My warmest regards to Paul Meurice. Has Auguste come back?

XXXV.

To THE SAME.

BRUSSELS, 1*st July*, [1852].

A line in haste, dearest. Having no messenger, I send it by post. This very day a volume of mine has gone to press in London. *No one has dared to buy the manuscript;* it is being printed, that is all they have ventured to do in England.

It will appear on the 25th of July, and will be called *Napoléon le Petit*. It is about the size of *Le Dernier Jour d'un Condamné*.

I wrote this book after you left us.[1] I shall publish

---

[1] Mme. Victor Hugo had spent a few days in Brussels at the beginning of June.

the history of the Second of December later. Being obliged to postpone it, I did not want Bonaparte to profit by the delay. I hope that you will all like *Napoléon le Petit*. It is one of my best things. I wrote it in a month, working almost night and day.

The great business in London is going on satisfactorily. The capitalist has been found, but he wants to confine himself to literature. They are afraid of democracy in England.

Charles is writing his novel, and *working hard*. I am very pleased at this.

Do not mention *Napoléon le Petit* to any one, except Auguste and Paul Meurice; and beg them to say nothing about it. It must fall like a bombshell.

I have a great many things to say to you, but the post is going. Farewell for the present. I love you all.

XXXVI.

To Mme. Victor Hugo.

Brussels, 13*th July*, [1852].

Yesterday there was an incident. A deputation of exiles begged me not to leave Brussels. I replied: "It does not rest with me; I shall be expelled." "Wait till you are expelled," was the reply. I said to them: "But if we make a scandal of it, which may be a useful political step, there will be joint responsibility; you will, perhaps, all be expelled." "Well, we will follow you, and rally round you again in Jersey. If you leave, the exiles in Belgium lose their leader. The party, which is now in Brussels, will be shifted to London. You are the centre. In Jersey you will be isolated. Stick to us until you are expelled." I told them that I was quite at their service; and I begged them to reflect, for a general expulsion would be against the interests of many, especially the poorer ones. They are going to consult together again, and will come back.

My departure from here is none the less certain, — for the Lehon ministry will certainly expel me, — but, being no longer voluntary, it will be delayed for a few days.

You will have heard that in the papers here and in Germany I have been made senator, prince, and grand eagle of the Legion of Honor, with an allowance of two millions, in return for which *Napoléon le Petit* is to remain unpublished. I shrugged my shoulders. Then they talked about an amnesty.

Charles is finishing his novel. He read me the first chapters, which are admirably done. It is very remarkable, as regards both style and matter. I have no doubt whatever of its success, and I think you will be pleased.

XXXVII.

To THE SAME.

25th July, Sunday morning, [1852].

The printer has just left me, dearest. The book will appear on Wednesday or Thursday at the latest. You must start, therefore, as soon as you receive this. Go straight to Jersey, to Saint-Helier, which is the principal town. There must be good hotels there. You will take up your abode there, and await us. Charles has not finished his book, but is determined to start with me. I expect we shall be in Jersey by Friday or Saturday at the latest, as we intend to rush through London.

Dearest, before the week is over, I hope we shall see each other and be together again. It will be a real happiness, the first after these seven months of exile. My dear little Dédé, how glad I shall be to embrace you.

A number of incidents have happened and are still happening, and a violent Bonapartist storm will burst over the book. This is a matter of course. I will tell you the details when we meet.

You must have spent a happy week at Villequier. A portion of my heart lies buried there. Dearest, you went to see Didine's and Charles's grave; you prayed for yourself and for me, did you not?

As one must be prepared for everything, and incidents may delay us, do not be uneasy if we should not arrive in Jersey by the end of the week. I firmly believe, however, that we shall.

My fellow-exiles did not want me to go. Three deputations came to see me about it. I explained to them that my forced (inevitable) expulsion would mean honor for me and loss of prestige for them. They withdrew their objections, but I am glad to see that they are sorry to lose me, and that all of them, or nearly all, love me, and would be ready to rally round me. I know what I want, and I want only what is right.

I hope that I shall find Auguste in Jersey, and am delighted to hear what you tell me of the intended visit of Paul Meurice and his charming wife. We shall perhaps have some quiet days there, in spite of the tumult that is raised around my name.

Ponsard has been to see me. Janin has been, and

he shed tears when he embraced me. I believe I shall leave a good impression here, and that my memory will be respected.

I have only space left to send my fondest love to you and my Dédé.

XXXVIII.

To Mme. Victor Hugo.

London, 2d *August*, [1852].

Here we are in London, dearest. I am writing in great haste. Charles and I left Brussels the day before yesterday; my fellow-exiles had given me a farewell dinner the evening before. The following day several of them, among others Madier-Montjau and Deschanel, escorted me to Antwerp; there our fellow-refugees in Antwerp were awaiting me; they gave me a reception, and a banquet was arranged at which I took the chair. Yesterday the Belgian democrats of Antwerp entertained me at a grand luncheon to which they invited all the exiles.

Just as we were sitting down, a number of representatives and refugees from all parts of Belgium arrived to bid me farewell, among them Charras, Parfait, Versigny, Brives, Valentin, Etienne Arago, etc., — Agricol Perdiguier, Gaston Dussoubs, Buvignier, Labrousse, Besse, etc., had already come to Antwerp for the same purpose, and a lot of exiled writers and journalists, — Leroy, Courmeaux, Arsène Meunier.

Bocage came expressly from Paris. The whole journey was one long ovation.

When I left, Madier-Montjau addressed me in a really fine speech, which came from the heart. I spoke pretty well in reply. Then came speeches from the writers, from the representatives, from the Belgians, among them Cappellemans, whom you saw at Paul's and who made some touching remarks. When I embarked for London on the Ravensbourne at three o'clock, the quay was covered with an enormous crowd, the women were waving their handkerchiefs, the men were shouting, *Vive Victor Hugo.* I had tears in my eyes, and so had Charles. I replied, *Vive la République,* which produced a still louder burst of cheering.

At that moment came a pelting shower of rain, which, however, did not disperse them. All remained on the quay as long as the steamer was in sight. Alexandre Dumas' white waistcoat could be distinguished in the middle of them. Alexandre Dumas was kind and charming up to the last minute. He insisted on being the last to embrace me. I cannot tell you how deeply all this manifestation touched me. I saw with joy that I had sowed some good seed.

Madier-Montjau and Charras begged me, on behalf of all our fellow-exiles in Belgium, to see Mazzini, Ledru-Rollin, and Kossuth here, to settle the interests of European democracy with them. They said: "Speak as our leader." This will keep me in London till Wednesday. So expect us in Jersey on Thursday or Friday.

I hope that you are fairly comfortable there, and that before long you will be quite so. Charles is developing amid all this; he is going ahead in a thoroughly manly fashion.

If Auguste is with you in Jersey, it will be a great pleasure to me to embrace him. I wrote to Victor to be there by the 5th, and I count on it. We shall then be the old happy group.

My book will not appear till Thursday. There have been delays enjoined by prudence which I will explain to you. I am going to give the first five hundred francs which it will bring in to the exiles' fund.

I embrace you, my dearest wife. I embrace my Dédé, whom I have not seen for eight months. Alas, yes, it will be eight months to-morrow. What happiness! To meet again!

III. LETTERS FROM EXILE.
1852–1870.

I.

To M. LUTHEREAU, *at Brussels.*

JERSEY, 15*th August*, 1852.

HERE we are, my dear friend, in a delightful spot; everything is lovely and charming. You pass from a wood to a group of rocks, from a garden to a reef, from a meadow to the sea. The inhabitants are well disposed towards refugees. You can see France from the coast.

I shall write soon to my excellent colleague Yvan. He ought to look us up in Jersey. We would spend a year there and then go to Madeira or Teneriffe together. After which M. Bonaparte would fall and all of us would return to France singing a final chorus. Tell him of this plan.

To-morrow I move with my family into a pretty little house which I have taken, near the sea. My address now will be: St. Luke's, 3 Marine Terrace. But there is no need to put an address. All letters directed simply to Jersey reach me.

II.

To ANDRÉ VAN HASSELT.

JERSEY, 15*th August*, 1852.

I am enveloped in poetry, dear poet, amid rocks, meadows, roses, clouds, and the sea, and naturally my thoughts turn to you.

What fine lines you would write if you were here! They spring as it were of themselves from this splendid scenery. When the view is not grand, it is lovely.

To-morrow I take up my abode in a little den near the sea, which the newspapers of the island describe as a " superb house on the Azette shore." It is a cottage, but the ocean lies at its foot.

We talk about you among ourselves; my wife and my daughter read your fine works, which I brought them. Charles and I tell them of our expeditions to Louvain, to Hal, in your company. We miss you; we long to have you.

About ten or twelve miles from here there is a huge rock, an island called Sark. It is a sort of fairy palace full of marvels. A man named Ludder or Lupper has just bought the manorial rights of it for £6000. Here is one of those cases in which poets envy millionaires. I should like to buy such an island and give it to Mme. van Hasselt. She would be obliged to come there. We should have your pleasant talk, dear poet. And I should still be the richer of the two.

III.

To ALPHONSE ESQUIROS.

MARINE TERRACE, *5th March*, 1853.

Are you still in Belgium? Are you still at Nivelles? I write to you at random. My thoughts often turn to you. You must feel it. Your letter of the end of December moved me deeply. It seemed to me like a greeting from our youth, with a tenderness refined by exile.

You are one of the men whom I love the most and the best. You have all the great beliefs in the future and in progress. You are a poet as well as an orator, with enthusiasm for truth in your mind, and a ray of the future in your eyes. Grow greater and greater; cultivate more and more your sympathy, your tenderness, and your firmness. Let us one and all, militant minds and consciences weighed down with this age of struggle and transformation, accept the great law which presses on us without crushing us; let us hold ourselves ready for the future evolutions of events and things; let us belong to the people now and prepare for belonging to humanity in the future.

I write all this as my mind runs on, at random, as it comes to me, somewhat as the ocean flings its waves, its weeds, and its breezes. Come and look at our Jersey sea, if you go to Portugal this spring. I am assured, and I can well believe it, that Jersey is a paradise in April. It is melancholy and gloomy in winter, but the summer makes up for this. Come to us, dear poet, with April, with the dawn, with the spring, with the songs of the birds.

I have spent my winter in writing some sombre lines. They will be called *Châtiments.* You can guess the subject. You will read them one of these days. *Napoléon le Petit* being in prose was only half of the work. The wretch was roasted on one side only; I turn him over on the gridiron.

Oh, my dear comrade in thought and in action, let us not lose heart. Let us persist, let us struggle on, let us redouble our efforts, let us persevere in the war against unrighteousness, hatred, and darkness.

IV.

To ANDRÉ VAN HASSELT.

MARINE TERRACE, 11*th May*, 1853.

It will be a year to-morrow, dear poet, you recollect and I do not forget, since we went to Hal together; it was raining a little, but we did not notice the cloudy sky and we did not feel the cold wind as we listened to your talk. We went to see the marvels of ancient art together, we bought the Catholic knickknacks and the pictures of miracles sold at the church door, and Charles and I shocked you a little by laughing at the miracles inside. I believe, heaven help me, that I managed, like a demagogue that I am, to count the stone balls which the black virgin received so opportunely in her apron.

Now I am far away; I see no miracle but the continuance of the hideous reign of crime and fear. The beautiful church and the charming poet are no longer there, but I think of you, and through space, over sea, sky, cloud, wind, and tempest, I send you my thoughts.

I also send you a picture of myself and one of Charles, done by my other son Victor. The door behind us is the small door of our tiny house. In these three square inches you have the exile and his cottage.

What you do not have, what could not be contained in such a small space, what I cannot send you, for words are powerless to express feelings, is my deep and tender friendship for you. I divide it in two and lay one half at the feet of your charming wife.

You have read fragments of the speech.[1] I send you the whole of it. Do not be distressed, but rejoice that the victims preach magnanimity to the persecutors. It is a noble sight, and worthy of your mind.

v.

To NOËL PARFAIT.

MARINE TERRACE, 29*th October*, [1853].

What has become of you? What has become of Brussels? What has become of the Boulevard Waterloo? As for Dumas, we hear of him. Every morning we get a sparkling page which tells us that the kind heart and the great mind are well. Your last letter delighted us, dear exile; it was a delicious little private diary, resembling your smile. Charles said: " C'est Parfait." And we all repeated the pun with which Providence has connected you.

You had, about two months ago, a delightful evening fête. The *Presse* related it to us from the *Indépendance Belge* (article signed with a capital D, and written by a charming fellow called Deschanel); then the said fête came back to us from New York quite fresh through the *Républicain*, from California through the *Messager* of San Francisco, from Rio Janeiro through the *Cor-*

[1] A speech over the grave of a refugee.

reio Nacional, and from Quebec through the *Moniteur Canadien*. Tell Dumas, so that he may see that his fêtes are as successful as his books. Tell Deschanel, too, who will not be sorry to have been reprinted by the four points of the compass.

The equinox is blowing with force here; but it makes no difference, we live in profound calm. The skies weep; the sea howls among the rocks; the wind roars like a wild beast; the trees writhe on the hills; Nature rages around me. I look her full in the face, and say to her: What right have you to complain, Nature; you who are in your abode, while I who have been driven from my country and my home, I smile! There is my dialogue with the north wind and the rain. Make use of it in your turn as opportunity offers.

The book [1] I have told you about is at last going to appear. When you see all my dear friends, — Charras, Deschanel, Place, Laussedat, Labrousse, Madier, our brave and eloquent Madier, — greet them for me.

VI.

To MLLE. LOUISE BERTIN.

[1853.]

Remain the great mind that I have known.

Remain the same great heart and great soul.

The success of the moment is nothing. Justice and truth are everything.

You are capable of comprehending the grandeur of the struggle of right against crime; of the idea against brute force; of the thinker against the dictator; of the moral atom against material iniquity. You are capable

[1] *Les Châtiments.*

of comprehending this; you do comprehend it, I am certain. Do not write in such a way as to inspire doubts of it.

Yes, we suffer.

We suffer and we smile.

If these men did not suffer, where would their merit be? If they did not smile, where would be their grandeur?

Remain yourself. Cherish the proud isolation of your mind. That certain men should surround you is intelligible; but that they should influence you, no, never! Do not permit it. You are too high for that. It is the triumph of small minds to mount on the shoulders of superior minds. Do not allow them these familiarities. . . .

Do not, with your virile intelligence, sink into the monarchist trifling. Look at the real future. Your eyes are strong enough to gaze steadfastly at that sun. . . .

VII.

To EMILE DESCHANEL, *at Brussels.*

MARINE TERRACE, *Sunday, 11th December,* [1853].

Will you still object? Am I right in calling you my poet? Do you know that your lines are superb? The close is marked by an energy *qui vous sacre brun, ou même noir.* "Sacrebrun" will, perhaps, make you say "sacrebleu." But what do I care? Swear, if you like. Your lines delighted us. Charles claps his hands, Toto drums with his feet, Vacquerie embraces you.

The Jersey papers quote from every part of the book,[1] and are full of it; and, oddly enough, the Eng-

[1] *Les Châtiments.*

lish papers themselves quote it in French. They say that the lines are untranslatable, which made an English lady here ask the other day *if they were obscene.* I replied: Not a doubt of it; the Bonaparte is in every line.

How I should like to be among you again, if it were only for an hour. Do you still dine at the Aigle? Do you remember Charles's tirades against the white asparagus? and that excellent faro![1] and our pleasant talks! and our hearty laughter! And our long discourse on the soul and on God, which we put off to another day, which has never come! And your course of lectures, as the climax of all! I can see you now at the end of the large room, which was not large enough, seated in your chair with the light on you, — gentle, pleasing, modest, applauded, charming, — surrounded by a crowd of men whose hands clap, and by pretty women whose hearts beat. . . . My mind goes back to those days as it does to my native land.

Here, in winter, everything is sombre, dark, violent, terrible, tempestuous, severe. The rain pours down my window-pane like a stream of silver; all nature plunges with frenzy into the tumult, and I have little to do but to storm like the wind and roar like the sea.

When you see our convalescent Hetzel, who makes his pallor an excuse for his laziness, tell him to write to me. Say bravo to Dumas from me for two delightful numbers of the *Mousquetaire*, which have reached my den. And you, think of me; write me a nice long letter, marked by that charming feeling, that exquisite style, that profound and gentle mind, which is applauded at Brussels and loved in Jersey.

[1] The beer drunk at the Aigle.

VIII.

To VILLEMAIN.

19th March, 1854.

... No, my friend, I have no personal complaint to make. I thank God for all that He has been pleased to do with me, for the ordeal which I undergo, for the desolation amid which I meditate. I welcome adversity, welcome injustice, welcome hatred, welcome calumny, which creeps into the exile's life like the worm into the sepulchre. If all these things which the world has agreed to call misfortune, and which I bear, add a single grain to the sum total of human progress, I bless destiny.

. . . .

Do you know what Jersey is? Take a map of the Archipelago and look out Lemnos. There you have Jersey. By the most capricious chance imaginable, God has made the same island twice over; He has given one to the Greeks, the other to the Celts. Jersey, placed on the top of Lemnos, would fit it almost exactly.

It is from there that I write to you; not from the island where the lightning is made, but from the island where it is expected. For sooner or later upon such things and such men the thunderbolt must surely fall. . . .

IX.

To DAVID D'ANGERS.

MARINE TERRACE, *26th April,* 1854.

DEAR GREAT DAVID, — I have received your kind and noble letter, with the interesting page which it contained. I am glad that you liked the book.[1] Dear friend, envy me, all of you, envy me; my exile is good, and I thank destiny for it. In these days, I do not know if proscription means suffering, but I know that it means honor. O my sculptor, one day you put a wreath on my head, and I said to you: Why? — You foresaw my proscription.

Talking of this, I am sending you that masterpiece, and I intrust it to your care. I have no home, the bust is expelled like the man. Open your door to it. I hope that one of these days, soon perhaps, I shall come and fetch it. In the mean while, keep it for me.

And keep your brave and generous friendship for me. I press your hand, poet in marble.

X.

To EMILE DESCHANEL, *at Brussels.*

MARINE TERRACE, *Sunday,* 28*th May,* [1854].

Now you are happy, dear gentle poet; and, although the rain and the wind are descending on my head, although the mist has spread a gray covering over the sky and the sea, although in my garden, which is invaded by my neighbor's poultry-yard, I see only geese and not a single bird, although these horrible geese are at this very moment engaged in rooting up and eating seven shillings' worth of French beans which I sowed last week, in the midst of all this unpleasantness and all these calamities I feel your happiness bringing me warmth and smiling at me from a distance, and my heart is full of joy.

As soon as you have received and read this letter,

[1] *Les Châtiments.*

take your charming wife on your knee and say to her: Somewhere in the world, in a remote spot, far away from here, there lives a sort of morose old creature, a dreamer of dreams, a dealer of blows to the right and to the left, an owl who is the sworn enemy of counterfeit eagles; this gentleman thanks you, madam. — Your wife will say: And for what? You will reply: For my happiness.

Yes, madam (I resume), I thank you for loving this kind heart, this charming mind, this untrammeled thinker, this generous poet; I thank you for having discovered all his worth, and for having said to yourself: Nothing is lacking to him; he is an exile.

Your letter, dear poet, reached us that very Tuesday, the 23d. I said to myself: It is impossible to go and dine there. And so to make up for it I drank, we all drank, your health. My wife sends her love to yours.

It is very nice of you to have remembered me when you were finishing your course of lectures. They will be resumed in the Grande Place. How I should like to be at No. 16 again! But alas! Napoleon the Little has driven me out of Brussels. Up to now this is his only exploit. And who knows if I shall not be one of those who will drive him out of Paris?

I will conclude with this pleasant idea and with a kiss on both cheeks, *i. e.*, one on yours and one on Mme Deschanel's.   V. H.

Make haste, make haste with the little promised Deschanel!

XI.

To ALEXANDRE DUMAS.

MARINE TERRACE, 17th *November*, 1854.

MY DEAR DUMAS, — A friend has cut four lines out of a number of your *Mousquetaire* and sent me them. In these four lines you have managed to put two great things, your mind and your heart.

I thank you for dedicating your drama *La Conscience* to me. My solitude had some claim to this remembrance. The dedication, so noble and so touching, makes me feel as if I were home again. It is a delight to me to think that I am in Paris now, and connected with a success of Alexandre Dumas. I am told that the success is great and the work profound. They resemble my friendship for you.

Dear comrade in action, great and glorious colleague, I embrace you.

XII.

To MME. DE GIRARDIN.

MARINE TERRACE, 4th *January*, 1855.

The year 1855 has had a daybreak for us, — your letter. It came full of radiance, like the dawn, and, like the dawn, with some tears. In reading it I seemed to see your beautiful tranquil face which resembles hope. All Marine Terrace was illumined for a moment as by a flash of joy. . . .

I am in no hurry, for I am much more concerned with the morrow than with to-day. The morrow should be formidable, destructive, reparative, and always just. That is the ideal. Will it be attained? All that God does is good; but when He works through man, the tool sometimes goes wrong and plays tricks in spite of the workman. Let us hope, however, and prepare. The Republican party is ripening slowly, in exile, in proscription, in defeat, in trial. There must be a little sunshine in adversity, since it is the latter which makes the crop grow and fills the ear of corn in the mind of man.

I am therefore in no hurry, I am sad; it pains me to wait, but I wait, and I find that waiting is good. What preoccupies me, I say it once more, is the enormous revolutionary continuation which God is now bringing on the stage behind the Bonaparte screen; I kick holes in this screen, but I do not wish God to remove it before the appointed time. You are right, however, the end is visible even now: 1855 can have no other issue than 1812; Balaklava is the same as Beresina; the little N. will fall like the great one in Russia. Only the Restoration will be called Revolution. Your name is Madame de Staël as well as Madame de Girardin; you are not Delphine for nothing, and, with the charming indifference of a heavenly luminary, you shed your rays upon the cesspool.

You have all the success that you wish for; yesterday in Molière's house, to-day in M. Scribe's.[1] It suits you to raise vaudeville to the rank of comedy, and you do it, and Paris applauds, and Jersey recommends Guyot to pocket a good round sum in author's dues, which will perhaps bring the muse to this Carpentras of the ocean. For you half promise it to us; do not forget this detail, I beg. In the mean while our Carpen-

---

[1] *La joie fait peur*, at the *Comédie Française*, and *Le chapeau d'un horloger*, at the *Gymnase*.

tras gives balls, at which your flowers produce a great effect. Your bouquet and my daughter danced together, the one wearing the other, and quite astonished the English, whose taste for pleasure has not yet been destroyed by the Crimea. I am told that Paris is not so frolicsome, and I can understand it. Disgrace is even sadder than misfortune.

For the rest, a belief in the speedy fall of M. B. is in the air; I hear it from all sides. Charles said just now as he was smoking his cigar: "*1855 sera une année œuvée.*"[1]

I talked about you yesterday with Leflô, who admires and adores you, a complaint he has caught from Marine Terrace. As he often comes to see me, this leads to his letters being opened in Paris, and some time ago the prefect of police is said to have sent one to the Minister of War, who showed it to Number III., who read it, and said: "Why, Victor Hugo has made a Red of Leflô." Leflô repeated the remark to me; I congratulated him on it.

Ten months hence you will have the *Contemplations*.[2] Send me your new success. You will find inclosed in this the speech you mention, which has made a stir in England and has drawn down upon me a threat in Parliament, to which I have rejoined. I send you my rejoinder in this envelope.

The tables[3] do in fact tell us some surprising things. How I should like to talk with you, and kiss your

[1] Literally, a year with eggs: a year big with promise for the future.
[2] The volume of poetry which Victor Hugo was then writing.
[3] Table-turning, which Mme. de Girardin had introduced into Jersey, and which was greatly interesting the inmates of Marine Terrace just at this time.

hands, your feet, or your wings! Did Paul Meurice tell you that a whole quasi-cosmogonical system, hatched by me and half committed to paper for twenty years, had been confirmed by the tables with splendid amplifications? We live in a mysterious landscape which opens out new prospects, and we think of you, to whom we owe this glimpse into another world.

The tables enjoin on us silence and secrecy. You will therefore find nothing from them in the *Contemplations*, with the exception of two details, of great importance, it is true, for which I have *asked permission* (I underline these words), and which I will indicate by a note.

XIII.

To EMILE DESCHANEL, *at Brussels.*

MARINE TERRACE, 14*th January*, 1855.

I am working almost night and day, I am sailing in a sea of poetry, I am faint with excess of light; hence my silence, dear poet, but I love you.

Your reproaches are just, charming, and unjust. I think of you very often. On Wednesday evenings I fancy that I have a little more leisure than on others; and then my flesh says to my spirit, How stupid you are! it is too far to go to his lecture this evening.

You are my neighbor, however; you are now splendidly lodged in the Grande Place where I made my nest for seven months, between the lofty belfry full of memories of the Duke of Alba and the inkstand out of which issued *Napoléon le Petit*. Do you remember? You used to come in the mornings; Charras sat in one corner, Lamoricière in another, smoking Charles's pipe; Charles and Hetzel on the sofa which served me for a bed; and with the sunshine streaming into my broad window, I read you a page or two of the book. What hearty shakes of the hand we gave each other afterwards!

Now all has assumed other colors, rosy for you, sombre for me. You are married to success, to happiness, to a charming wife, to an enamored public, to applause, to smiles; *I* have wedded the sea, the hurricane, a vast sandy shore, sadness, and the starry canopy of heaven.

I wish you a happy New Year, madam, with two countries and two men, Belgium plus France, and your husband plus a son. Write to me, dear friend, break in upon my reveries with that merry, unaffected laugh of yours that I like so much. We expect the little Franco-Belgian at the appointed time. We know that you take good aim.

I accept your two kisses and send you four in return, one on each cheek. V. H.

Tell my excellent friend Hetzel that I am rowing hard in his direction. The *Contemplations* will be an exceptional book. If ever there was a mirror of the soul, it will be this.

XIV.

To MLLE. MARIE HUGO[1] (SŒUR SAINTE-MARIE-JOSEPH).

JERSEY, 22d *July*, [1855].

I thank you for your present, dear child. Your little painting is charming; the pink color is like your

---

[1] A young relative of the poet, who took the veil when her husband died a year after their marriage.

face and the dove like your soul; it is almost a painting of yourself that I have, pending the arrival of the other. You have promised it, and I am anxious to have it.

The lines which you sent us this spring were very graceful; there were some very sweet and happy stanzas on you especially. Tell this from me to the writer of them, who must be charming if she is like her poetry.

Dear child, so you are about to accomplish the solemn act of leaving the world. You too are going into exile; you will do it out of faith as I have done it out of duty. One sacrifice can understand another. Therefore it is from the depths of my heart that I ask for your prayers and send you my blessing.

I should have liked to see you once more on that last day for family meetings of which you tell me. God does not permit us this happiness; He has his ways. Let us be resigned. I will send the angel whom I have above to visit you. All that you are doing for your brother is good; I recognize in it your devoted, noble heart. Dear child, you and I are in the sweet and austere path of renunciation; we are nearer to each other than you imagine. Your serenity comes to me as a reflection of my own. Love, believe, pray; be blessed.

XV.

To MICHELET.

MARINE TERRACE, 24th *July*, 1855.

You have received the same blow as I have. To-day death pays a sudden visit to your house as it did to mine twelve years ago. You have lost your child, your daughter, your darling, and you are in tears. I shed the same tears as you, and that is all that I can offer to your sorrow. O great mind, you are now bleeding from the heart. It is only the heart which really bleeds. All other sufferings are nothing in comparison. To lose one's child is real misfortune. There is no such desolation or exile in life as this.

I say nothing to a soul like yours. You, who will be one of the founders of the earthly kingdom, you cannot doubt of the heavenly kingdom. <u>I believe in God because I believe in man.</u> The acorn proves to me the oak, the ray the star; that is your symbol, and mine. We shall meet those who are dear to us hereafter; your daughter is now by the side of mine; henceforth these angels smile on us and illumine us; and even without your knowing it there are more gleams of light within you. This brightness comes from death. Dear and glorious fighter of the human fight, poor father, I embrace you.

VICTOR HUGO.

I have just read some admirable pages of yours. But is this a time to speak to you of glory? Yes, for your glory is "a soldier of God," and is ever in attendance on human thought. Let your labors, which are your crown, be your consolation.

XVI.
To GEORGE SAND.

4th August, 1855.

I hear that a calamity has befallen you. You have lost a little child. You are suffering.

Will you allow one who admires you and loves you to take your hand in his and to tell you that you have all his sympathy? Your grief is mine, for the same reason that makes your success my happiness. Great soul, I suffer in you.

I believe in angels; I have some in heaven, I have some on earth. Your little darling is now a sweet winged soul, hovering o'er your illustrious head. There is no death. All is life, love, light, or waiting for the light. I offer you my tender respect. I regard you with sincere affection.

XVII.
To MME. VICTOR HUGO.

GUERNSEY,[1] 3 P. M., [1855].

Here we are on land, dearest, not without some tossing. The sea was rough, the wind boisterous, the rain chilly, the fog thick. Jersey is not so much as a cloud even; it has disappeared; there is nothing on the horizon. I seem to be in a state of suspended animation; when you are all here, life will begin again.

---

[1] Victor Hugo, having been expelled from Jersey for siding with the other refugees, had sought shelter in Guernsey, and preceded his family there.

The reception was good; there was a crowd on the quay, silent, but sympathetic, apparently so at least; all took off their hats as I passed.

I have a grand view before me as I write. Even in the rain and fog the approach to Guernsey is splendid. Victor was greatly struck by it. It is a regular old Norman port with hardly anything English about it.

The consul with a white tie on (the Laurent of this place) was present when I landed. Somebody told me that he raised his hat like the others when I passed.

It seems that the local authorities have said that we shall be unmolested here, provided we do not create any difficulties. We are looked on as malefactors. But volcanoes are not to be extinguished with pails of water.

XVIII.

To Messrs. Thomas Gregson *and* Joseph Cowen, *of Newcastle, Members of the Foreign Affairs Committee.*

Guernsey, Hauteville House, 25*th November*, 1855.

Dear fellow-countrymen of the great fatherland of Europe, I have received from the hands of our brave co-religionist Harney the communication which you have been so good as to address to me on behalf of your committee and of the meeting held at Newcastle. I thank you, as well as your friends, for it, in my own name and in that of my fellow-combatants and fellow-exiles.

It was impossible that the expulsion from Jersey, that this proscription of the proscribed, should not excite public indignation in England. England is a great and generous nation, which throbs with all the living forces of progress; she understands that liberty means light. But what has just been done in Jersey is a night attack; it is an invasion of darkness; it is an armed assault by despotism on the old free Constitution of Great Britain; it is a *coup d'état* insolently launched by the Empire in the heart of England. The expulsion was carried out on the 2d of November; that is an anachronism, it should have taken place on the 2d of December.

Pray tell my friends of the committee, and your friends of the meeting, how much we were touched by their noble and energetic manifestation. Such acts may serve as a warning and a check to those of your rulers who are perhaps, at this moment, meditating a fresh attack on the old honor of England, through the shameful Alien Bill.

Demonstrations like yours, like those which have just taken place in London, like those which are in preparation at Glasgow, consecrate, draw closer, and cement, not the idle, spurious, baneful, effete alliance between the present English cabinet and the Bonapartist empire, but the true, necessary, eternal alliance between the free people of England and the free people of France.

XIX.

To FRANZ STEVENS, *at Brussels.*

HAUTEVILLE HOUSE, 10*th April*, 1856.

Your name, so young and yet assured of fame, has a sort of radiance for me. The first time I heard it I was arriving in Brussels; it was the 13th or 14th of December, 1851; some lines were placed in my hands; my name was at the head, yours at the foot. These lines — the first that you wrote, I believe — revealed at that early stage all that was in your heart. You arose on the threshold of your native land to greet the man who had no other refuge but the great fatherland which is called exile; and you offered the refugee the hospitality of poets, which is more to be depended on than that of kings. This was a fine beginning. It has brought you good fortune. From that day onward your poetical gift has grown, and to-day it is my turn to bid you welcome on the threshold of that other land of refuge, art. Five years ago you nobly connected my name with lines which were a wreath of laurels; allow me to-day to tell you in prose that I love you.

You are not a Belgian poet, you are a French poet. You have the grace, the brilliance, the life, the originality in details, the felicity of expression, the ease, the freedom of movement, the proud bearing of the French writer. The union of Belgium with France is thus accomplished by writers and poets. You are one of those who generously fling between the two nations the splendid connecting-link of style, of poetry, of the winged strophe, of the idea.

You and I belong to different political regions. You, at this moment, are where I have been. Perhaps your mature age will reach the point where I am now, including proscription, which I hope may be your lot. You deserve it; for whatever the formal disagreement which separates us, you want all that we do, we the champions of the right; you wish for enlightenment, truth, progress, the interment of the past, the advent of the future; you wish to see the end of misery, of ignorance, of perdition, of servitude, of darkness; you desire, under the sole authority of God, the sovereign ego in the free individual. This is the kernel of your ideas; the outer husk will fall from it.

You and I, therefore, are the same man; we touch each other; you are what I was in the past, I am what you will be one day. You are to me the mirror of what I was; look at me and think of your future.

Within a given time your reason will accomplish the first task, and your conscience the second; and, after all, it is better that corrections should be effected by them. What these inner workers bring about and rectify is always the best part of us. I content myself with applauding, with crying bravo to your beautiful and noble lines; with encouraging your brave and energetic mind; yes, bravo and courage! I am not a French writer welcoming a Belgian poet. I do not belong to the former nation, and you do not belong to the latter; for me, in politics there are only men, and in poetry poets; and whatever standpoint I adopt, I can only see in you a brother.

I write this to you somewhat promiscuously, somewhat at random. Try to realize the state of my mind in the splendid solitude in which I live, perched as it were on the summit of a rock, with all the grandeur of the waves and the sky before me. I dwell in this immense dream of the ocean. I am gradually becoming a somnambulist of the sea; and in face of all these stupendous phenomena and all this vast living thought in which I lose myself, I end by being only a sort of witness of God.

It is from this never-ending contemplation that I

arise to write to you. Therefore take my letter as it is, take my thoughts as they come, — somewhat disconnected, somewhat disarranged by all this gigantic oscillation of the infinite. What is fixed and steadfast is the soul in presence of God, and conscience in presence of truth; and also — and I will end by this — the profound sympathy with which young men like you inspire me.

XX.

To VILLEMAIN.

9th May, 1856.

I read your letter with emotion. We start almost from two opposite poles in art, but grief has given us a great trysting-place in truth, and I am not surprised that we should meet. You refresh your mind — that delicately chased Greek goblet — at the sacred limpid springs from which human thought filters and falls drop by drop throughout the ages. *I* am in the wilderness, alone with the sea and with grief, drinking from the hollow of my hand. Your drop of water is a pearl, mine is a tear.

But you, too, have wept; you, too, have suffered; you, too, are bleeding. Hence the deep sympathy between us; deeper than we are ourselves aware of, and which is as it were revealed to us at certain moments. You have read *Horror, Dolor*,[1] and you have recognized the distant sound of the bell which all sufferers and thinkers hear in the night.

Dear friend, I often think of you. Exile has not only detached me from France, it has almost detached me from the earth; and there are moments when I

[1] Two pieces in the *Contemplations*.

feel as if I were dead, and when I seem to be already living the great sublime life beyond the tomb. It is then that my thoughts revert to all those whom I have loved in this world below. . . .

XXI.

To LOUIS BOULANGER.

HAUTEVILLE HOUSE, 24*th May*, [1856].

What a precious possession, dear Louis, is the enduring warmth of old friendships! Your letter seemed to bring back my youth. *Je nous ai revus,* — this jargon just expresses my thoughts, — in the glorious days of the *Orientales,* when we were two passers-by on the plain of Vaugirard, two watchers of the sun setting behind the dome of the Invalides, two brothers, you the dazzling painter of Mazeppa, I the dreamer predestined to strife and exile.

You are happy now; you say so in your letter. I feel it and I love you.

You have read that book, and you know my feelings by it. I know yours by the way you speak to me of it. I should now like to make the acquaintance of your wife; I am sure she is noble and charming. In my eyes you shine as it were in a soft halo; you seem to me to have kept your youth. And I, from the depths of the vast darkening twilight which enfolds me, send you and her, dear Louis, my fondest and tenderest greeting.

XXII.

To BARTHÉLEMY ENFANTIN.

GUERNSEY, *7th June*, 1856.

I thank you, dear and great thinker; your letter touches and charms me. You are one of the seers of the universe. You are one of those men in whom humanity is stirring, and with whom I feel a profound sympathy.

The ideal is the real. Like you, I live with my eyes fixed on a vision. I do my best so far as my strength will allow to help mankind, that hapless crowd of brothers we have there who are walking in darkness, and I endeavor, bound to the chain myself, to aid my fellow-travelers, by my example as a man in the present, and by my writings as a poet in the future.

Within due limits, my sympathy embraces all created beings. I see your point of view, and I accept it, and I think you will also accept mine. Let us work towards the light. Let us create unbounded love.

In those two books, *Dieu* and *La Fin de Satan*, you may be sure that I shall not pass over woman; I shall go even further, just as I shall go beyond the things of this world. These two works are almost finished; nevertheless, I want to leave an interval between them and the *Contemplations*. I should like, if God gives me some measure of strength, to carry the crowd to certain altitudes; yet I am well aware that there is little air there which it can breathe. I therefore wish it to rest awhile before I make it attempt a fresh ascent.

Alas! I am of very little account, but my heart is filled with deep love for liberty, which is man, and for truth, which is God. You have this twofold love as well as I; it is the life of your lofty mind; and it is a pleasure to me to greet you as a friend.

XXIII.
To George Sand.

15th June, 1856.

Guernsey should be called Tibur, Ferney, or Port Royal, to be able to send a fitting reply to Nohant. But Guernsey is only a poor rock, lost in the seas and in the darkness, bathed by the spray which leaves on the lips a salt taste of tears, with no merit but its cliffs and the patience with which it bears the burden of the infinite. The little sombre island is proud of the ray of sunshine which comes to it from Nohant, the birthplace of beautiful and charming books. Alas! sorrow is everywhere, the grave is everywhere, but the light is where you are! I thank Heaven if my book has been able to touch your grief without wounding it, and if it has been vouchsafed to me — to me who am sad myself — to bring some balm to the anguish of your large heart, O great thinker, O poor mother!

Victor Hugo.

XXIV.
To the Same.

Hauteville House, 30th June, 1856.

You have every gift; the greatness of your mind is only equaled by the greatness of your heart. I have just been reading your splendid article on the *Contemplations*, that criticism which is poetry, that flow of thought, of life, and of tenderness, that philosophy, that reasoning, that gentleness, that powerful and striking exposition, those gems which drop from a pen of light. What is there for me to say? To thank you is almost stupid; I would rather congratulate you. You are a serene nature; you are proud because you are high-minded; you speak of this book[1] with a calm simplicity, and so genuine as to be almost haughty, when one compares it with the wretched clevernesses of so many other minds. I said of you to my children one morning at breakfast, — this is our *autour de la table,* — that in the world of thought you were the greatest of women, perhaps even of all time. . . .

You are a dweller on the heights, and you are accustomed to eyries; I have only a den. But I should like you to come and see it; let me roll away the great stone at the entrance and bid you enter.

To drop metaphor and in plain prose (how can I venture to use this epithet to you who write such grand prose?), with the proceeds of the first two editions of the *Contemplations* I have just bought a hovel here; I am going to improve it and add to it; and there will then be a decent room for you; will you make up your mind to come? It will be about next spring; you see I give you a long notice. It is a way of making it almost impossible for you to refuse. You will be in my house what you are in your own, that is to say, free. The house shall have the name "Liberty;" it will be called *Liberty House*. It is the custom in England to give houses names. As you perhaps know, my family and I live in the most simple manner, and in this respect Guernsey can join hands with Nohant. Think over it, you have nearly a year before you, and

---

[1] George Sand had written several articles on the *Contemplations*.

come to us. If you only knew how sincerely I mean this invitation! You will walk in my garden, a very small one; do not expect your vast plains. There is so much sea and sky here that one hardly needs a bit of earth.

My wife has already invited you: you half promised her to come; complete the promise to me. It will give us a pleasure on which we shall live till we see you. You will write a splendid book here and date it from Guernsey; be kind to this poor old rock and confer on it this distinction. I have marked it with a period of ordeal, do you mark it with one of glory.

One thing pleases me, and that is that my book *Dieu* (three parts finished) anticipates your ideas. It seems as if you must have read it when you wrote that letter from Louise which concludes your admirable articles. The end full of light, that is what I desire and you desire, and the good Theodore himself (I know many such) will be satisfied.

You are an *esprit;* consequently I say to you familiarly, Thanks. And you are a woman, which gives me the right to kneel before you and respectfully to kiss your hand.

XXV.

To GEORGE SAND.

HAUTEVILLE HOUSE, 2d *October*, 1856.

It is a joy to me to think that your great mind turns now and again towards mine; and when I find my name in your noble articles, it seems as if they were open letters from you to me. I should think myself an ungrateful being if I did not reply to them. However, you do not need thanks or applause. In this age, when almost every one is more or less insincere, you have the proud, simple bearing of a genuine character. In my solitude this communion of our souls, I may almost say of our hearts, makes me silently and profoundly happy. I feel as if I were linked to you in the contemplation of truth and the acceptance of sorrow; and I hail your serene and impressive testimony in favor of progress. Whoever despairs of man despairs of God, — that is to say, does not believe in Him. And all religions in the present day are atheistical; all curse the light, — that is to say, the very dawn of the heavenly countenance. *You* have faith because you are great. I thank you, I admire you, and, allow me to add, I love you.

XXVI.
To THE STUDENTS OF PARIS.

1856.

Young and courageous fellow-citizens, your noble and cordial letter has reached me in my solitude, and has touched me deeply. I have very little time to myself; exile is no sinecure, as you are aware; and I take the first opportunity at my disposal to reply to you and to thank you. Courage, and persevere.

The eyes of the future rest on such as you. Among the signatures to the valuable letter which I receive, I see some which represent talent, others which represent example; all represent generosity, intelligence, and moral worth. Your trials are beginning early; rejoice in it. Your sufferings nobly borne place you at the head of your generation. Be always worthy of directing it. Let nothing unsettle or discourage you. The future is certain. Wait for it amid the affliction and darkness of the present moment as one waits for the dawn in the night, with quiet and perfect faith. Work and advance; think, and you will discover; struggle, and you will conquer.

I greet you all as I would my brothers or my children.

XXVII.

To EDMOND ABOUT.

HAUTEVILLE HOUSE, 23d *December*, [1856].

Exile has but little leisure, and it is only here in the sort of temporary lull which always follows a renewal of persecution, that I have at last been able to read your two fine and charming volumes, *Tolla* and *La Grèce*. My sons, your old school-fellows, have often mentioned you to me. You have achieved all that they prophesied of you, and I congratulate you with all my heart. You are gifted, you are successful, you are young; your responsibility for others is beginning.

An outlaw is a sort of dead man; he can almost give advice from beyond the grave. Be faithful to all those great ideas of liberty and progress which are the very breath of the future for all humanity, for the people as well as for the genius.

Despise all that is not true, great, just, and beautiful. Your nature is an enlightened one. I need only say to you: Be true to yourself.

Take courage, then. You are entering bravely and successfully into the future.

XXVIII.

To ALEXANDRE DUMAS.

HAUTEVILLE HOUSE, 8*th March*, 1857.

DEAR DUMAS, — The Belgian newspapers bring me, with all the splendid comments which you deserve, the letter which you have just written to the director of the *Théâtre Français*.

Great hearts are like great suns. They contain their own light and warmth. You have no need, therefore, of praise; you do not even need thanks; but I must tell you that I love you more every day, not only because you are one of the marvels of the age, but also because you are one of its consolations.

I thank you.

But pray come here; you know you promised to do so. Come and receive the greetings of all who surround me, and who will not gather round you less loyally than round me.

Your brother.

XXIX.

To GEORGE SAND.

HAUTEVILLE HOUSE, 12*th April*, 1857.

Daniella is a great book and a beautiful book; allow me to tell you so. I do not touch on the political side of the work, for the only things that I could write about Italy could not be read in France, and would probably prevent my letter from reaching you. I am speaking to you, to you the artist, about the work of art. As for all the great aspirations towards liberty and progress, they are necessarily part of your nature; and a poetical genius like yours is always on the side of the future. The revolution is light, and what are you but a torch?

I look on *Daniella* as a profound study of all the aspects of the heart. It is masterly because it is womanly. You have put into this book all that feminine delicacy which, blended with your masculine power, makes up your strong and charming individuality. As a painter I would stand up for all the old ruins of Italy against you; and in particular for that dazzling and imposing Campagna of Rome which I saw as a child, and which has remained in my mind and become impressed on my vision as if I had beheld a mixture of sunshine and death. But what does this matter to you? You continue your course full of light and inspiration; you scatter around you brilliant, generous, cruel, gentle, tender, haughty, smiling, consoling pages, and you know that, after all, the sympathies of every reader are with you as a writer, just as all minds are fascinated by your intellect.

So accept my homage with that of the rest. My house is nearly finished, and humbly hopes to receive you; and I respectfully kiss your hand.

XXX.

To ARSÈNE HOUSSAYE.

HAUTEVILLE HOUSE, 16*th January*, 1858.

Your letter, my dear poet, has just reached me through our Brussels friend. It touches me deeply. You have, like me, your beloved grave, your dear spirit, your never healing wound. Between our souls is the great link of a common sorrow. When the blow fell on you, I thought of you, I recalled that charming woman, now a spirit. Alas! to lose those we love is the only real sorrow; all the rest is nothing; I have said so in the book of which you speak in such high terms.

Take courage; you have all the great consolations of poetry and art, and who should hope more than the poet? *Hecho de esperar*, as Calderon says.

XXXI.
To GEORGE SAND.

HAUTEVILLE HOUSE, 28*th May*, 1858.

Do you ever happen to think of me a little? I fancy it must be so, for I glide so gently and naturally into thoughts of you.

I have just been reading *Les beaux messieurs de Bois-Doré*, and every time I read one of your books my heart expands with joy. I delight in all the strength, in all the grace, in the beautiful style, in the lofty mind, in the charming discoveries on every page, in feeling the throbs of the powerful philosophy underneath the caressing poetry, and in finding such a great man in a woman. Permit me to tell you that my sympathies are entirely yours.

My house is still but a hovel; it has been taken possession of by worthy Guernsey workmen, who, believing that I am grand, think themselves justified in making a little money out of "the rich French gentleman," and in prolonging the work and the profit. I imagine, however, that it will be finished one day; and that then, perhaps, in some time or other, you will take a fancy to come to it, and consecrate a small corner of it by your presence and your memory. What do you say to that illusion?

What a treasure illusions are! I love them, but I love realities still more, and a woman like you is a glorious reality in an age. Write, console, instruct, continue your grand work; live amongst us with the indulgent serenity of great affronted souls.

XXXII.

To JULES SIMON.

HAUTEVILLE HOUSE, 25*th June*, [1859].

Your fine book *La Liberté* has been a long time in reaching me, and I have spent a long time in reading it and meditating on it. Do not be surprised, then, at my slowness in thanking you for it; I do not apologize for this; the delay is of small importance: works like yours can afford to wait, because they will last.

It is almost a code that you have written; from one end to the other there is a genuine breath of legislation.

It has often happened to me in reading your works to feel the kind of surprise and delight that one experiences on finding one's own thoughts admirably expressed by another person. Your chapter on property, in particular, is one of the profoundest and most telling parts of your book. It is a great gift, and you possess it, to be able to enforce irrefutable theories by a captivating style. These two volumes, in which history is so powerfully appealed to in support of philosophy and facts in support of ideals, will rank as a great work. You have selected the right moment for defending liberty; there is no better time than the darkness for glorifying the light.

XXXIII.

To ADÈLE HUGO, *in London.*

21st July, 1859.

You are wrong, dear child; a smile and a kiss from you are more precious to me than all the flowers here below and all the light from above. I long to see your mother and you again; my birthday is a sad affair nowadays: last year illness and this year absence.

However, if you both return in good health, I shall think that all is for the best. But you have chosen a bad time for your trip; I hear on all sides that London is infected and poisoned by the Thames in the summer; the papers are full of horrid details of the cleansing process which has been necessarily suspended. So make haste and get out of that fever-den.

All is well at Hauteville. Charles is resting, Lux[1] reflecting, Toto[2] grinding away, Chougna[3] meditating, I am working, the garden perfumes the air. I assure you we have roses coming into bloom which look as if they would outlast the Palmerston Ministry, and that we too have a first-rate concert, *gratis*, of waves, of breezes, and of birds. Beethoven's is the only music I could listen to after that which I have here.

I hope, dear child, that you too will get to like it some day, and that, with your fine feeling for melody and harmony, you will not always be insensible to the great symphony of God.

My garden is the dress circle at that opera. Come back to it, my beloved daughter, with your dear mother, as soon as possible. I embrace you both tenderly.

[1] Charles Hugo's dog. [2] François Hugo. [3] Victor Hugo's dog.

XXXIV.

To GEORGE SAND.

HAUTEVILLE HOUSE, 21*st August*, 1859.

Will you allow me to remind you that I am still your slave? It is in my nature to persist, and at any rate it is not in my admiration and tender respect for you that I could fail. Do not therefore put down my long intervals of silence to forgetfulness.

I work and meditate in my solitude, and I think of the noble minds who, like you, fan the flame of the great Vestal called the Idea in France. Yes, you have the ideal within you; pour it forth, pour it on the hapless multitude of to-day steeped in materialism and brutality; discharge your august function of priestess, and you will earn my heartfelt thanks.

As I am writing to you, I will not conclude without inclosing some lines which I cannot publish in France, and which you will readily understand, on the last piece of insolence of this wretched *réussisseur*.[1]

When will you come to illumine my darkness? — Dear and great mind, I love and venerate you.

XXXV.

To VILLEMAIN.

HAUTEVILLE HOUSE, 17*th November*, 1859.

DEAR FRIEND, — Do you know what exile means? It means waiting for six months to hear words uttered by you, who are one of the illustrious speakers of the age. A friend from Paris came to see me yesterday.

---

[1] The amnesty proposal of 1859, rejected by a number of exiles with Victor Hugo at their head.

He had the happy idea of putting into his trunk your book on Pindar, and since yesterday I have done nothing but read that excellent and profound work. I bathe in Pindar and in you as in a life-giving stream. You translate Pindar as you feel him, as you interpret him, powerfully, and when I say Pindar, I include Æschylus, Sophocles, Aristophanes, Horace, all those divine genuine poets. Their spirit has completely saturated yours. Your prose does not clip those grand wings.

The reason is that with the noblest instincts and the most steadfast courage you combine the flame of enthusiasm. Your book is a history in which at times one feels the throb of poetry. The last few pages are a splendid ode to the future.

I do not perhaps agree with you on every point, but that is of small importance. I regard your book as I do you, with profound esteem. An occasional greeting from you, in the Chamber, or at the Academy, or by the fireside, is one of the pleasures of my native land which I miss the most.

In two passages of your fine book you allude to me with a sort of tender emotion which goes to my heart. I thank you. I have been resting in you for the last few hours as in a haven of the mind. I need these periods of rest sometimes in my solitude, in face of the ocean, amid this sombre scenery which has a supreme attraction for me, and which draws me toward the dazzling apparitions of the infinite. Sometimes I spend the whole night meditating on my fate, before the great deep, and at times all I can do is to exclaim: Stars! stars! stars!

Your book is one of those which gently produces a

change of ecstasy. Instead of the sea-eagle, I watched Pindar soar. I listened as you narrated — and with what exalted eloquence! — the history of enthusiasm, that is to say, of human genius. And in the way in which you pronounce that lofty and enchanting word, "Liberty," I recognized the very echo of my soul.

I press your two hands in mine, my illustrious friend.

XXXVI.

To ALEXANDRE DUMAS.

HAUTEVILLE HOUSE, 11*th December*, 1859.

It is you, dear Dumas, whom I must congratulate on your son's last success [1] and on all his successes. How truly admirable and delightful! the father partaking of the fame of the son, the son sharing in the glory of the father.

Yes, you are indeed a *père prodigue;* you have given him everything, striking situations, ardent passion, lifelike dialogue, sparkling style; and at the same time — a miracle quite simple in art — you have kept everything; you have made him rich without impoverishing yourself.

And he, on his side, manages to be original, while remaining your son; he is you and he is himself. Pray embrace him for me.

I also, *anch' io,* have sons who make me happy (and, I add in a whisper, proud, for we fathers are obliged to be modest about our children), and it is as a proud father that I congratulate you, the glorious one. But let this be said discreetly and between ourselves.

So you are starting. If I were Horace, how I would

---

[1] Alluding to the performance of *Le père prodigue.*

sing to Virgil's ship! You are going to the land of
the sun, to Italy, to Greece, to Egypt; you will sail
on sapphire waters, you will behold the smiling sea.
I remain in the gloomy one. My Ocean envies your
Mediterranean. Go, be radiant, be great, and come
back. *Te referent fluctus!*

Your friend.

XXXVII.

To GEORGE SAND.

HAUTEVILLE HOUSE, 20*th December*, 1859.

I thank you for your delightful and grand words.
You speak to me of the *Légende des siècles* in terms
of which Homer would be proud. I am pleased that
this book has arrested your bright steadfast gaze for a
few moments.

Just now I am overwhelmed with grief. They have
killed John Brown. The murder took place on *the 2d
of December*. The promised respite was an infamous
device for lulling popular indignation. And it is a
republic which has done this! What sinister folly it
is to be an owner of men; and see what it leads to!
Here is a free nation putting to death a liberator!
Alas! my heart is indeed sad. The crimes of kings
one can understand: a king's crime has nothing abnormal about it; but crimes committed by a people
are intolerable to the thinker.

I am reading your admirable letter over again with
delight and consolation. You too have your trials.
For me, who often gaze at you, they enhance the sweet
and lofty calm of your countenance.

I respect and admire you.

XXXVIII.

To HENRI DE LACRETELLE.

HAUTEVILLE HOUSE, 4*th February,* 1860.

There is no consolation, dear poet, for grief such as yours. Alas! that charming woman, that flower of your youth, that dawn of your life, that luminous vision of our past, has really gone! She was a sweet apparition, she is now a spirit. We are born to lose all that is best here below. It is seventeen years ago that an angel I had, my daughter, departed; but I have her still; I cannot see her, but I feel her in my life, and I await her when I die. You too now turn your thoughts in this direction. It is the law of life. We must die successively in all those whom we love, to live again in them hereafter.

You have all the great and serious interests of poetry and art; your noble mind will heal the wounds of your broken heart.

Courage, dear poet. I press your hand tenderly.

XXXIX.

To THÉCEL, *of the Indépendance Belge.*

February, 1860.

I have just read a delightful article of yours, brilliant and serious at the same time, on George Sand's tales of rural life. I commend you heartily, and I thank you for having praised George Sand, especially at the present moment. There is an unsatisfactory tendency just now to disparage her great reputation and eminent talents. The first symptoms of this somewhat virulent epidemic appeared several years ago.

True, no one understands and admits more readily than I do the lofty and serious criticism to which Æschylus, Isaiah, Dante, and Shakespeare themselves have to submit, and which has the same rights over the spots in Homer as the astronomer has over the spots on the sun; but the fierceness of literary hatreds, the rancor of men against a woman, and even assize court rhetoric directed against a high-minded and illustrious writer, these I do resent; they surprise and offend me deeply.

George Sand is a luminous heart, a beautiful character, a generous combatant on the side of progress, a light of our age; she is a far more genuine and powerful philosopher than certain good people who enjoy more or less notoriety just at the present moment. And yet this thinker, this poet, this woman, is the victim of a sort of blind and unjust reaction! I repeat the word reaction, for it has several meanings, and includes everything.

For my part, I have never felt more disposed to honor George Sand than now when she is being insulted.

XL.

To CHAMPFLEURY.

HAUTEVILLE HOUSE, 18*th March*, 1860.

I hasten to answer your affectionate letter. The undertaking you have in hand, successfully carried out by a man like you, cannot but promote the intellectual movement now in progress.

Art is not perfectible; that constitutes its greatness, and that is the source of its eternity (I use this word of course in the human sense). Æschylus remains Æschylus, even after Shakespeare; Homer remains

Homer, even after Dante; Phidias remains Phidias, even after Michael Angelo. Only the appearance of Shakespeares, of Dantes, and of Michael Angelos is not limited; the constellations of yesterday do not block the path of the constellations of the morrow; and for a good reason, because the infinite cannot be crowded. So forward! there is room for all. We cannot surpass geniuses, but we may equal them. God, who has created the human brain, is inexhaustible and fills it with bright luminaries.

As long ago as 1830 I said, rejecting all appellations which are transitory and which characterize nothing: The literature of the nineteenth century will have but one name; it will be called democratic literature. It will have but one aim: the increase of human enlightenment through the combined action of the real and the ideal.

The novel is almost a conquest of modern art; the novel is one of the forces of progress and one of the resources of human genius in this great nineteenth century; and you, by the precision as well as the elevation of your mind, are one of the masters of it.

XLI.

To M. HEURTELOU, *editor of the Progrès at Port-au-Prince* (*Haiti*).

HAUTEVILLE HOUSE, 31*st March*, 1860.

Your letter touches me. You are a noble specimen of that colored race which has been so long oppressed and misunderstood. From one end of the earth to the other the same flame burns in man, and you are one of those who prove it. Was there more than one Adam?

Philosophers may discuss the question, but what is certain is that there is but one God. As there is but one Father, we are all brothers. It was for this truth that John Brown died; it is for this truth that I fight. You thank me for it, and I cannot tell you how much your noble words move me. There is neither black nor white in the world, there are spirits only; you are one of them. All souls are white before God.

I love your country, your race, your liberty, your republic. Your beautiful island has an attraction just now for free spirits; she has just set a great example: she has crushed despotism.

She will help us to crush slavery. For slavery will disappear. What the Southern States have just killed is not John Brown, but slavery.

Henceforth the American Union may be looked on as broken up. I deeply regret it, but it is a foregone conclusion. Between the North and the South there is the gibbet of John Brown.

Joint responsibility is no longer possible. The burden of such a crime cannot be borne by two persons. Continue your task, you and your worthy fellow-citizens. Haiti is now a centre of light. It is a grand thing that among the torches of progress which light the path of mankind, one should be seen in the hands of the negro.

Your brother.

XLII.

To the Members of the Committee *for erecting a monument to Ribeyrolles, at Rio-de-Janeiro.*

4th *November*, 1860.

Gentlemen, — Ribeyrolles sought a home with you, and he wrote a fine book about you, a book worthy of your noble nation, of your illustrious history, of your beautiful country. He noted with enthusiastic sympathy your more and more enlightened advance in the direction of progress. He has done fraternal justice to you in the name of democracy and civilization. Many pages of his book are like marble tablets on which your glory is written, on which your future is predicted. He died at this task, he died an exile, he died poor; you Brazilians owed him a debt; you have decided to repay it in a splendid fashion.

Ribeyrolles had erected a monument to Brazil; Brazil raises a memorial to Ribeyrolles. All honor to you! To receive in this way, and to make such a return, is doubly admirable.

You desire an epitaph for his tomb, and it is to me that you apply; you ask for my signature on the monument. I am deeply sensible of the honor you do me. I thank you for it.

From the dawn of history, two sorts of men have led mankind : the oppressors and the liberators. The former sway it for evil, the latter for good. Of all liberators the thinker is the most effective; his action is never violent; the mildest of powers, and consequently the greatest, is the mind. The mind inflicts deadly blows on evil. Thinkers emancipate the human race. They suffer, but they triumph; they accomplish the salvation of others by the sacrifice of themselves. They may die in exile; but no matter, their ideal survives them, and continues after their death the work of liberty they began during their life.

Charles Ribeyrolles was a liberator.

The emancipation of all peoples and of all men, — that was his aim. Humanity free, the nations brothers, — that was his sole ambition.

This rooted idea, which was destined to end in his exile and his glory, is what I have tried to set forth in the six lines which I send you, and which you can engrave on his tomb if you think fit.

For my part, I rejoice in the appeal which you make to me. I respond to it with alacrity. You are noble men, yours is a generous nation; you possess the double advantage of a virgin soil and an ancient race; you are linked to the great historical past of the civilizing continent; you mingle the light of Europe with the sun of America. It is in the name of France that I honor you.

Ribeyrolles had done this before me. He had greeted you with all his eloquence; he commended you, and he loved you. You honor his memory, and you do well. It is the great brotherhood of mankind asserting itself; it is the meeting of two worlds around the bier of an exile; it is Brazil shaking hands with France across the ocean.

Accept my thanks! Ribeyrolles, in fact, belongs to you as he does to us; such men are common property; even their exile has the merit of bringing into relief this universal brotherhood; and when despots rob them of their native land, it is a grand thing that peoples should give them a tomb.

I greet you and I am your brother.

VICTOR HUGO.

À CHARLES RIBEYROLLES.

Il accepta l'exil ; il aima les souffrances ;
Intrépide, il voulut toutes les délivrances ;
Il servit tous les droits par toutes les vertus ;
Car l'idée est un glaive et l'âme est une force,
 Et la plume de Wilberforce
Sort du même fourreau que le fer de Brutus.

XLIII.

To M. CHENAY.

HAUTEVILLE HOUSE, 21*st January*, 1861.

DEAR MONSIEUR CHENAY, — You expressed a wish to engrave my drawing of John Brown,[1] and now you desire to publish it; I consent, and I add that I think it desirable.

John Brown is a hero and a martyr. His death was a crime. His gibbet is a cross. You remember that I wrote at the foot of the drawing: *Pro Christo, sicut Christus.*

When in December, 1859, I predicted to America with deep sorrow the rupture of the Union as a consequence of the murder of John Brown, I did not think that the event would follow so quickly on my words. At the present moment all that was in John Brown's scaffold is issuing from it; the latent fatalities of a year ago are now visible, and from henceforth the rup-

---

[1] Victor Hugo had made a large and splendid drawing representing John Brown on the gallows, with the inscription, *Pro Christo, sicut Christus.*

ture of the American Union, a great calamity, is to be dreaded; but the abolition of slavery, an immense step in advance, to be hoped for.

Let us then once more call the attention of all to the gibbet of Charlestown, as a lesson, and as the point of departure of these grave events.

My drawing, which your fine talent has reproduced with such striking fidelity, has no value but in its name of *John Brown,* a name which must be continually repeated, — to the republicans of America, to remind them of their duty, to the slaves, to summon them to freedom.

XLIV.

To M. CRÉMIEUX.

BRAINE-L'ALLEN, 28*th May*, 1861.

DEAR FRIEND, — I have received your letter of the 25th of March; *but it did not reach me till to-day, the 28th of May.* On the 25th of March, I left Guernsey, being unwell and in search of change of air; for the last two months I have been moving from one town to another, enjoying the pleasures of convalescence, and it is only to-day that I had the joy of reading your kind and charming letter. It touches me deeply. You are not only a man of eloquence and power, you are a good man. *Vir bonus* . . . and all the rest of the definition. I can hardly express to you how dear you are to me, how fond we all are of you. I, your client, and my son Charles, your other client, are always talking of you. No one is more eloquent than you; no one has a loftier soul. This is natural, however; it is the soul which inspires the voice.

I am quite well again. I shall return to my rock

very soon. If ever some good star were to bring you there, oh, my dear visitor, how glad I should be to receive you in my poor abode! It would be a red-letter day for all the refugees, and you would gladden our exile as you console the fatherland.

Lay at your daughter's feet the autograph she is good enough to ask for. I was a long time thinking over a phrase to write at the foot of this portrait, which should express everything of which Mademoiselle Crémieux is entitled to be proud, and at last I found it. Here it is : —

To the daughter of Crémieux.

I press your hand, my noble and generous friend.

XLV.

To MESSRS. GIUSEPPE PALMERI, LUIGI PORTA, SAVERIO FRISCIA, *Members of the Italian Managing Committee, at Palermo.*

BRUSSELS, 21*st June,* 1861.

GENTLEMEN, — In your eloquent letter, which touches me deeply, you inform me that my name has just been inscribed on the list of the Association for Italian Unity by the spontaneous and unanimous decision of the whole society.

I accept with pleasure the place which you offer me among you. As far as my duty to democracy will allow I shall warmly second your efforts. You thank me in a grand fashion for the little I have done ; such thanks are a reward.

Members of the Italian Committee, your undertaking is a sacred one. The restoration of a great people is more than a restoration, it is a resurrection. All the forces of progress converge on the aim which you pursue, and assist you. In founding Italy, you are not laboring solely for your own country, but for the world. United Italy is necessary to civilization.

The great Europe of the future is already beginning to take shape. The tendency of peoples is to group themselves in races, as a preliminary to grouping themselves in continents. These are the two phases of civilization which are logically linked together, the one leading up to the other: first national unity, then continental union. These two steps in advance will be the achievement of the nineteenth century; it has already nearly accomplished the first, it will not come to a close without having accomplished the second.

A time will come when frontiers will cease to exist. All wars will disappear in the fraternity of races. That will be the great day of the human fatherland.

Pending the realization of these sublime changes of the future, continue, persevere, advance; let all men of intelligence and feeling do the duty of the moment; let each nation demand its unity, the necessary contribution of each people to the great federal compact of the future; let a lofty political philosophy inspire and transform diplomacy itself; let whoever mutilates or diminishes a people be outlawed by humanity. Let us all be fellow-countrymen in progress, and let us all repeat, from the European as well as from the Italian point of view: Italy must have Venice and Rome, for without Venice and Rome there can be no Italy, and without Italy there can be no Europe.

XLVI.

To EMILE DE GIRARDIN.

LONDON, 16*th August*, [1861].

I am in London, staying at an inn; a newspaper has just been brought me, the *Presse;* I find in it your name, which I am always looking for, and my name, which you are fond of writing. You are right; if we could have a free discussion in public, we should soon agree; you are a follower of the radical and I of the ideal. Well, the root is the idea.

But it is no use your being Girardin and Voltaire being Voltaire; both Voltaire and Girardin are obliged to make concessions, and must always, to obtain permission to speak, be scattering the word *king* here and there in their most logical and most unanswerable arguments, as Spinoza scatters the word *Christianity*. Well, in philosophical radicalism the word *Christianity* is only a drop; in political radicalism the word *king* is only a drop; but a drop of arsenic, mixed with the best beverage in the world, makes it difficult to digest.

When the day comes for you to be free, your grand logic will burst forth in all its fullness, and will bring out the accuracy of your profound mind. On that day we shall evidently, I imagine, be agreed on almost all points. In the mean while, you are obliged to accept the men of the Empire, and the Empire within certain limits, just as Orpheus accepts Cerberus in order to pass him; and you throw them your noble style as a sop. They will let you pass, but you will return alone, and they will not let you bring back the Eurydice called Liberty. A serpent has stung her in the heel, and a demon guards her in the sepulchre.

All the same, I am glad to have a talk with you. You are in my eyes one of the great servants of progress, of truth, of logic, and of liberty; our differences are only reasons why we should try to understand each other thoroughly.

XLVII.
To GEORGE SAND.

HAUTEVILLE HOUSE, 18*th February*, 1862.

Where are you? Where will this letter find you? At Nohant or in Paris? Do you sometimes think of a distant friend whom you have never seen, and who is sincerely and deeply attached to you? All the good, great, and beautiful things that you have done for all in this age — you, a woman, with your tenderness, you, a sage, with your love — make me one of your debtors, and amid the immensities which surround me, ocean, sky, stars, nature, humanity, storms, revolutions, I call to you and I think of you, and my spirit says to yours: Come.

I am overwhelmed with work and business, and in this predicament, with which you are familiar, when one has not a moment to one's self, a letter to write seems an aggravation; but it is a rest to write to you.

Your glory is one of those which shine with mild rays. The contemplation of a light such as yours is a joy to the soul.

When shall we be able to converse, and see each other, and tell each other all that we have to say? Alas! France seems to be receding from me; I only wish Guernsey could move nearer to you.

It seems to me that, if you liked, you are prophet enough to make the mountain come to you.

I kiss your hand, and I thank it and congratulate it on having written so many beautiful works.

XLVIII.
To GEORGE SAND.
HAUTEVILLE HOUSE, 6*th May*, [1862].

Your letter has made me sad. Imagine what a painful surprise it was to me. I had fancied that this book [1] would bring us still nearer to each other, and now I find that it estranges us, that it almost disunites us. I should be angry with the book if I were not convinced of its perfect sincerity.

Evidently one of us is wrong. Is it you? Is it I? As your outspokenness encourages mine, allow me to tell you that I think it is you.

I had dreamed that you, the great George Sand, would understand my heart as I understand yours. At any rate, living a solitary life, face to face with my intention and alone with my conscience, I am sure, if not of my achievement, at all events of my purpose; I am sure of my heart, which is the slave of justice, of the ideal, of reason, of all that is great, generous, beautiful, and true, of yourself.

XLIX.
To THE SAME.
HAUTEVILLE HOUSE, 18*th May*, [1862].

It is nice to be wounded by goddesses when one is healed by them. Thank you for your two exquisite and kind letters. Those who cannot be charming are

---

[1] The first part of *Les Misérables*. George Sand had given a qualified approval only to the saintly Abbé Myriel.

not great, and you prove this, for you are charming. Your greatness converts itself at will into grace, and it is in this way that it shows itself. . . . You who have strength, possess charm as well.

Do not be afraid of my becoming too much of a Christian. I believe in Christ as I do in Socrates, and in God more than in myself. I am more certain of the existence of God than of my own. If you go on with the book, read the part called *Parenthèse;* your anxiety about this imaginary apprehension of yours will be dispelled.

Let us change the subject to you. Now you are happy into the bargain. Your son, who has something of your genius, is going to be married. Be successful in Paris and happy at Nohant. Live in an atmosphere of glory; that is a fitting lot for you. I kiss your hands, and I thank you for your adorable letters. I perceive that I am in love with you. Luckily I am an old man!

L.

To LAMARTINE.

HAUTEVILLE HOUSE, 24*th June*, 1862.

MY ILLUSTRIOUS FRIEND, — If to be an idealist is to be a radical, then I am one. Yes, from every point of view, I understand, I desire, and I hail improvement; *le mieux*, though condemned in the proverb, is not the *ennemi du bien*, for that would be equivalent to saying that it is the friend of evil. Yes, a society which tolerates misery, a religion which admits hell, a humanity which admits war, appear to me to be a society, a religion, and a humanity of a lower order; and it is towards the society, the humanity, and the religion of a higher world that I aspire : society without kings, humanity without frontiers, religion without sacred books. Yes, I combat the priest who sells lies and the judge who administers injustice. To universalize property (which is the reverse of abolishing it) by getting rid of parasitism, *i. e.*, to achieve the following object, every man an owner of property and no man master, that is my idea of true social and political economy. To sum up, as far as a man can will it, I would destroy human fatality, condemn slavery, banish misery, enlighten ignorance, cure disease, illumine darkness, and detest hatred.

These are my principles, and that is why I wrote *Les Misérables*.

In my view *Les Misérables* is simply a book with fraternity for its starting-point and progress for its goal.

Now judge me. Literary disputes between persons who have received a literary education are ridiculous, but political and social discussion between poets, that is to say between philosophers, is serious and fruitful. Evidently your aims are the same as mine, to a great extent at least; only perhaps you would like to see the transition made still more gentle. For my part, while putting aside all idea of violence and reprisals, I confess that, seeing so much suffering, I am in favor of the shortest way.

Dear Lamartine, long ago, in 1820, the first lispings of my youthful muse were a cry of enthusiasm at the dazzling rise of your genius on the world. Those lines are in my published works and I love them; they are there with many others which glorify your splendid gifts. To-day you think it is your turn to speak of me, and I am proud of it. We have loved each other for forty years, and we are still alive; you would not wish to spoil this past or the future, I am sure. Do what you will with my book and with me. Nothing but light can come from your hands.

Your old friend, VICTOR HUGO.

LI.

To OCTAVE LACROIX.

HAUTEVILLE HOUSE, 30*th June*, 1862.

DEAR SIR, — I readily answer your letter, for I recognize in you a valiant combatant for truth and right, and I greet a noble mind.

After having, like you, fought against the Second of December, I was banished from France. I wrote *Napoléon le Petit* at Brussels; I had to leave Belgium. I went to Jersey, and there fought for three years against the common enemy; the English government was subjected to the same pressure as the Belgian government, and I had to leave Jersey. I have been in Guernsey for seven years. I have bought a house here, which gives me the right of citizenship and protects my person; here I am safe from a fourth expulsion. However, I am bound to say that Jersey two years ago, and Belgium a year ago, spontaneously reopened their doors to me.

I live near the sea in a house built sixty years ago by an English privateer and called Hauteville House. I, a representative of the people and an exiled soldier of the French Republic, pay *droit de poulage* every year to the Queen of England, sovereign lady of the Channel Islands, as Duchess of Normandy and my feudal suzerain. This is one of the curious results of exile.

I live a retired life here, with my wife, my daughter, and my two sons, Charles and François. A few exiles have joined me, and we make a family party. Every Tuesday I give a dinner to fifteen little children, chosen from among the most poverty-stricken of the island, and my family and I wait on them; I try by this means to give this feudal country an idea of equality and fraternity. Every now and then a friend crosses the sea and pays me a visit. These are our gala-days. I have some dogs, some birds, some flowers. I hope next year to have a small carriage and a horse. My pecuniary circumstances, which had been brought to a very low ebb by the *coup d'état*, have been somewhat improved by my book *Les Misérables*. I get up early, I go to bed early, I work all day, I walk by the sea, I have a sort of natural armchair in a rock for writing at a beautiful spot called Firmain Bay; I do not read the seven hundred and forty articles published against me during the last three months (and counted by my publishers) in the Catholic newspapers of Belgium, Italy, Austria, and Spain. I am very fond of the worthy, hard-working little people among whom I live, and I think they are rather fond of me, too. I do not smoke, I eat roast beef like an Englishman, and I drink beer like a German; which does not prevent the *España*, a clerical newspaper of Madrid, from asserting that Victor Hugo does not exist, and that the real author of *Les Misérables* is called Satan.

Here, dear sir, you have nearly all the details for which you ask me. Allow me to complete them by a cordial shake of the hand.

LII.

To Paul de Saint-Victor.

2d October, 1862.

I have just read your first article on *Les Misérables*. I thank you. For the last fourteen years, you have been writing, page by page and day by day, one of the great books of the age, the history of contemporary art confronted with the ideal. This serene comparison is the triumph of your luminous mind. Thought, poetry, philosophy, painting, and sculpture, you light up all with the splendid reflection of that vision of the beautiful which is within you.

And the charm of your soul is that it is a heart. In your artistic and philosophic teaching one feels the profound emotion of justice and of truth. With Æschylus you are Greek, with Dante you are Italian, and, above all, you are human. This makes you the profound thinker and the great writer whom I admire.

You know that not a line of yours escapes me. I read your works with the tender assiduity of a kindred spirit. At each stroke you hit the mark, and for many a year I have been following you with my eyes, and admiring you as one shaft after another from your inexhaustible quiver flies into the targets of the true and the beautiful.

To-day I am proud of the work which you link with mine. You inlay my wall with marble bas-reliefs. After reading the admirable article, in which every word has the profundity of the idea and the transparency of truth, I ought to have controlled my feelings, and held my peace until the series was finished and I could give you my impression of it as a whole. In future I will do so, but I was unable to do it on this occasion.

You forgive me, do you not?

Dear and great thinker, I press your hand.

LIII.

To MICHELET.

HAUTEVILLE HOUSE, 2d *December*, 1862.

I finished reading *La Sorcière* this morning, dear and great philosopher. I thank you for having written this fine work. In it you have depicted truth in all its aspects, of which, perhaps, the grandest is pity. You are not satisfied with convincing, you must touch your readers. This book is one of your great triumphs.

I love everything in it: the lifelike style, which suffers with the martyr; the thought, which resembles an expansion of the soul in the infinite; the large heart, the knowledge blended with emotion; the description, or rather the intuition of nature, from which issues the imposing figure of a sort of demon-god, who draws smiles and tears.

The hermit thanks you for having sent him this tender, deep, and poignant book. He is a melancholy dreamer, often sadly overwhelmed by the contemplation and the haunting thought of all the suffering in the world; but when his hand feels the pressure of yours, a ray of light seems to pass before his eyes.

LIV.

To EMILE DE GIRARDIN.

HAUTEVILLE HOUSE, 2d *April*, 1863.

The noise made by you people who are still in the world reaches my solitude late, but it does reach it eventually.

I learn that at a banquet of the *Presse* you had the splendid courage to evoke the absent, and that, in a toast of the noblest eloquence, you associated my name with that of liberty.

Liberty will not return under the present régime. It is afraid of her, and it is right; liberty has a good memory, and no cohabitation is possible between her and this government, born of sudden crime, the *coup d'état*, and upheld by a continuous crime, despotism. I do not share your hopes, and on the other hand my hopes might seem illusions to you; but we are agreed, you and I, in our devotion to progress and to that irreducible liberty, the vanquished of to-day, the victor of to-morrow.

LV.

To THE MEMBERS OF THE DEMOCRATIC CLUB OF PISA.

HAUTEVILLE HOUSE, 3d *April*, 1863.

MY ITALIAN BROTHERS, — Your eloquent and noble letter goes to my heart. I accept with alacrity the place which you offer me among you. Italy united and free is my wish, as it is yours. To liberate Italy is to add to civilization.

This very day, Friday the 3d of April, it is eighteen hundred and sixty-three years since Jesus Christ died upon the Cross. He did not die at Rome. He died at Jerusalem. It would seem that the Popes have forgotten this, since they have seated themselves on the summit of the Capitol without seeing that their place is at the foot of Calvary. Christianity is less august crowned in the Vatican than kneeling at Golgotha. A triple crown of earthly gratification and pride is a strange substitute for the crown of thorns.

Since the Popes harden their hearts, since they despise Jerusalem, since they usurp Rome, Italy too will harden her heart. Italy will resume possession of Rome, as a matter of right and duty. She will resume possession of Rome, as she will resume possession of Venice. The Pope, like the Cæsar, is a foreign sovereign.

LVI.

To LAMARTINE.[1]

HAUTEVILLE HOUSE, 23*d May*, 1863.

DEAR LAMARTINE, — A great blow has befallen you; I must bring my heart close to yours. I venerated her whom you loved.

Your lofty spirit sees beyond the horizon; you have a distinct vision of the future life. There is no need to say "hope" to you. You are one of those who know.

She is still your companion; invisible, but present. You have lost the wife, but not the soul. Dear friend, let us live in the dead.

[1] On the death of his wife.

LVII.

To GEORGE SAND.

TRÈVES, 26*th August*, 1863.

Forgive this dreadful hotel paper. I am traveling, and I write to you on the first table that comes handy. I am at Trèves, surrounded by all kinds of beautiful things, and how is it possible not to think of you? I have read the noble, charming, and cordial article which you have written on Mme. Victor Hugo's book.[1] It seems to me that henceforth the book is by you both; you countersign it, you magnify it by your glory. That is an illusion of the heart. Allow me to indulge in it.

You do not know how much I admire you. I take every opportunity of telling you so, and I thank you for giving me this one. There was, and perhaps there still is, something or other between you and me. But it has disappeared, or will disappear. The main thing for me is that I love you and understand you. You have a unique and exalted glory. You are the great woman of your age.

LVIII.

To THE MINISTER OF THE REPUBLIC OF COLOMBIA.[2]

HAUTEVILLE HOUSE, 12*th October*, 1863.

I cannot tell you how much your communication touches me. I have devoted my life to progress, and the starting-point of progress in the world is the inviolability of human life. The corollaries of this principle are the end of war and the abolition of the scaffold.

---

[1] *Victor Hugo raconté par un témoin de sa vie.*
[2] He had sent Victor Hugo a copy of the Constitution of Colombia.

The end of war and the abolition of the scaffold mean the suppression of the sword. The sword suppressed, despotism will vanish. It loses both its object and its means of existence.

You send me, on behalf of your free republic, a copy of your constitution. Your constitution abolishes capital punishment, and you are good enough to credit me with a share in this splendid reform. I thank the Republic of the United States of Colombia with deep emotion. In abolishing capital punishment it sets an admirable example. It takes two steps, the one in the direction of happiness, the other in the direction of glory. The high-road lies open. Let America advance, Europe will follow her.

Transmit, dear sir, my acknowledgments to your noble and free fellow-citizens, and receive the assurance of my high consideration.

LIX.

GENERAL GARIBALDI *to* VICTOR HUGO, *at Hauteville House.*

CAPRERA, 25*th November*, 1863.

DEAR VICTOR HUGO, — I was sure of your coöperation, you must be sure of my gratitude.

What you say is right, and I should like to have the million of souls which would enable me to dispense with the million of guns; I should like to see the universal agreement which would make war useless. Like you, I await with confidence the regeneration of peoples. But to realize truth without suffering, and to tread the triumphal path of justice without besprinkling it with human blood, is an ideal which has hitherto been sought in vain.

It is for you, who are the torch-bearer, to point out a less cruel way; it is for us to follow you.

Your friend for life,
GARIBALDI.

LX.

To GENERAL GARIBALDI, *at Caprera.*

HAUTEVILLE HOUSE, 20th December, 1863.

DEAR GARIBALDI, — We both of us have faith, and our faith is identical.

The regeneration of the nations is infallible. For my part, I have a profound conviction that, when the time has come, not much blood will be shed. The Europe of the peoples *farà da se*. Revolutions, even the most successful and the most necessary ones, bring their responsibility, and you, like me, are one of those who dread their having to bear the tremendous weight of one drop of blood too much. No bloodshed at all would be the ideal; and why not the ideal? When the ideal is reached in man, and you alone are sufficient to prove that this is possible, why should it not be reached in things?

Hatred decreases in proportion as the moral standard rises. Let us endeavor, then, to raise that standard. Emancipation by means of thought, revolution through civilization, that is our aim, yours as well as mine. And when the last fight has to be fought, there need be no anxiety, it will be beautiful, generous, and great; it will be as gentle as a fight possibly can be. The problem is in a way solved by your presence.

Dear friend, I press your illustrious hand.

VICTOR HUGO.

LXI.

To GEORGE SAND.

HAUTEVILLE HOUSE, 28*th March*, 1864.

I hear that you have returned to Nohant. That is where my applause likes to go in search of you. It is natural that one solitude should write to another. In your splendid triumph in Paris my voice would have been nothing; it is always of very little account in the blaze of fame which surrounds you; but it seems to me that down in the country, in the midst of your fields and your trees, you will hear it better.

My pleasures are but few; your success is one of them, and one of the best. You give our age an opportunity for being just. I thank you for being great and I thank you for being admired. In a gloomy period such as ours, your glory is a consolation.

LXII.

To LOUIS BLANC.

HAUTEVILLE HOUSE, 31*st March*, 1864.

MY DEAR LOUIS BLANC, — In the book which I am about to publish,[1] and in which I refer incidentally, and in high terms, to the committee,[2] I express myself against the idea of a subscription. A subscription is the ordinary accompaniment of this sort of manifestation. But for Shakespeare we want more than the ordinary. I think that the least which should be done for him is the vote of a great public monument by Act of Parliament.

---
[1] *William Shakespeare.*
[2] The committee formed in England for erecting a statue to Shakespeare.

This, in my judgment, is the direction which the action of the committee should take. Having expressed this opinion, which is about to be published, can I take part in the subscription? Can I write one thing and do another?

If it were a case which concerned the conscience, the immediate answer would be *No*. The present case admits of less strictness. Nevertheless, would there not be some inconsistency? You are on the spot, you have a near view of things; you combine ability with discrimination; allow me to appeal to you.

If you think that my book does not prevent me from subscribing, you can at once put me down for five pounds, and my son François Victor also for five pounds. If you think there is any drawback in my appearing to change my mind, and that I ought to hold aloof, I will do so.

My friendship asks permission to abide by the decision of yours.

LXIII.

To GENERAL GARIBALDI.[1]

HAUTEVILLE HOUSE, 24*th April*, 1864.

I did not ask you to come, because you would have come, and, however great might have been my joy at welcoming you — you, the real hero! — whatever happiness I might have had in receiving you in my house, I knew that you were better employed, and a man has not the right to take you from a people. Guernsey salutes Caprera and perhaps will visit it some day. In the mean while, let us love each other.

[1] Garibaldi was then in London receiving a triumphal reception from the English.

The English people presents a noble spectacle at this moment. Be the guest of England after having been the liberator of Italy; that is a grand thing. The man who is applauded is followed. Your triumph in England is a victory for liberty. The old Europe of the Holy Alliance is afraid of it.

The truth is that these cheers are a precursor of the deliverance.

XIV.

To CHARLES HUGO.

HAUTEVILLE HOUSE, [1864].

Your letter does not reply to the cry which came from the depths of my heart: Return!

We all miss you here, and I more than any one, as you are well aware. But I used the word "return" in every sense. I did not mean only return by the railway, I meant return by the heart; do not put an end only to the material separation which has so long parted us, put an end to the mental separation as well. You have caused me great pain, my poor dear child, but I forgive you because I love you, and when one loves, there is one thing which is impossible, and that is not to forgive.

Yes, my whole heart turns toward you and longs for yours. Return! return! Alas! while you are suffering at a distance, we are suffering too; you know my last tortures; that does not prevent me from being torn asunder by yours. You see, I was right; everything is happening as I predicted.

Ah, my God! to think of you so far away, so sad! What a crowd of troubles all at once! Return! return! I can say and think nothing else.

LXV.

To Mr. Tennant, *Glamorgan, Wales.*

HAUTEVILLE HOUSE, 15*th May*, 1864.

DEAR MR. TENNANT, — Before writing the book to which you draw my attention, you had done the following things.

You had poor laborers around you. You lent them thirty acres of your best land. You divided these thirty acres into allotments. Each allotment was large enough for two cottages and two good gardens. And you said to the poor people around you: Here is land for any one who wants it. The alignment must be followed, not more than two cottages can be built on one allotment; the rent of each allotment is a guinea a year, and I will give you a lease of a thousand years. In a few weeks all the allotments were taken up, hundreds of landowners were created, the scheme grew as time went on, and the result at the present day is a small town in Wales, in Glamorganshire, the town of Skewen. Every landowner in Skewen is a voter, *i. e.*, a citizen. You have made more than a town, you have made a city.

This is not all. You dug at your own expense a canal thirty feet deep and nine miles long, navigable for the largest vessels, and leading to the sea. The seaport is called Port Tennant.

A town called into being, a canal dug, a port built, is pretty well.

That, at any rate, is a good preface.

I am now reading your book, or rather I am having it read to me, for I do not know English.

I am more radical than you, as you are aware. You deal tenderly with parasitism; I would sweep it away. But, apart from this exception, I accept your book. Many of the expedients indicated by you are very ingenious, very elaborate, very efficacious, and are supported by principles. You sketch out, in sincere and powerful language, a juster apportionment of social burdens, a more normal distribution of territory, a more loyal civilization than ours, a better Europe. One day a better humanity will be your ideal. When that day comes you will understand everything; you will fight parasitism instead of regulating it; you will adopt, with all the energy of your upright character, and as an absolute and necessary starting-point of progress, gratuitous and compulsory education. Then you will be quite logical, — that is, on the way to the whole truth. Then your mind will be complete, and your books will be irrefutable.

In the mean while I content myself with all the excellent, just, true, and cordial things for the people in your book. The people suffers; let us love it. I do not say this to you, the founder of towns; I say it to every one. Let us love each other. One day in a sentence, I forget where, I had written the word *aimer;* the compositor put *aider*. I accepted this misprint. Let us love each other, and let us help each other. Let the rich love and help the poor; let the poor love and help the rich. All have need of all.

LXVI.

To GEORGE SAND.

HAUTEVILLE HOUSE, 17th *May*, 1864.

It is clear that being so great, you must be charming. Grace is a form of power. You prove this in all your works; you prove it in the exquisite and superb pages which I have just read. A friend has sent them to me. From henceforth he is more my friend.

I read what you have said, I read this grand and noble letter; it is written about me, and it seems to be addressed to me. I am deeply moved. What an inspiration of genius to have worked nature into the book; to talk of your life in the country in the same breath as art and science; to let the rustling of leaves and the twittering of birds be heard here and there amid the grand things which you say. Dante dictates one page, Virgil another. It is enchantment combined with strength. Ah, Circe! ah, George Sand!

I am very glad to have written that book, since it pleases you. So you like me a little? Really? Well, that was one of my ambitions.

I am very ambitious. I should like to see you. That again is a dream of mine. What a lovely portrait you have sent me! What beauty, dignity, and grave sweetness! Do not be afraid; I am an old fellow, and here is my portrait which proves it. I should like to be somewhere in the world, in a remote spot, — at Nohant, or Guernsey, or Caprera, — with Garibaldi and you; we should understand each other. It seems to me that we are three good specimens of this age. It is a thousand pities that I cannot go to Nohant. They tell me that

I am a voluntary exile. Parbleu! that is what keeps me here. If I had only Cayenne to fear, I should go to France whenever I liked.

Your letter converses. At the same time it is instructive, it is musical, it is meditative. The whole face of nature is reflected in a line of yours like the firmament in a drop of dew. You have vistas into the infinite, into life, mankind, the animal world, the soul. That is great. When a philosopher is combined with a woman, nothing can be more admirable. The deeper aspects are treated as well as the lighter ones. I am one of those who hold that the heart should think. You are that heart. Harmonious conversation is the conversation that I like; we should have it together, I fancy; our points of contact are numerous. Now I am boasting; smile and forgive me.

You will never grow old. You are ineffably gracious. While Paris applauds and adores you, you construct a little retreat in the depths of the country for yourself alone, and you fashion a shady nook in your glory. There are nests for souls as well as for birds. At this moment your soul is in its nest. Be as happy as you are great.

I close my letter in order to read yours again. I am told that there are people who envy my book. I do not doubt it; I am one of them; it has traveled with you, I am jealous of it.

I kneel before you and I kiss your hands.

LXVII.

To ALEXANDRE DUMAS.

HAUTEVILLE HOUSE, 16*th June*, [1865].

DEAR DUMAS, — I have just read your letter in the *Presse*. I read it without surprise. Nothing in the way of bravery astonishes me from you; and in the way of cowardice nothing astonishes me from these people. You are the light; the Empire is the darkness; it hates you, that is simple enough; it wants to extinguish you, that is not so simple. It will have its trouble for nothing. The shadow which it will cast upon you will only enhance your brightness.

A glorious incident for you, altogether, and honorable for me, and one on which I congratulate our old friendship.

LXVIII.

To GEORGE SAND.

BRUSSELS, 4*th October*, 1865.

I have been away and traveling about all the summer. I am passing through Brussels for the marriage of my son Charles, and am on the way back to my rock in mid ocean. Paul Meurice has been speaking to me of you, and I feel the need of writing to you. Will you allow me to tell you that I am devotedly attached to you? There are moments in life when sympathy, deeper and tenderer than ever, mingles with the admiration inspired by a great mind. That is the feeling which I send you; that is the sort of respect which I lay at your feet.

LXIX.

To THÉODORE DE BANVILLE.

CASTLE CARY, 25*th October*, [1865].

You answer my little familiar letters with splendid public replies. I have just read in the *Presse* your grand prologue to the *Chansons des Rues et des Bois*. It is the nightingale heralding the lark.

Since you are good enough to take a liking to this book beforehand, perhaps that will induce me to publish it. Your wish, dear poet, is a command to the muse.

Nevertheless, the sky is sadly overcast for committing this tiny bark to the winds and waves. I have my doubts.

I saw in the papers that I had been away from Guernsey *two months;* it should have been three months, and I am not back yet. I have been wandering about here and there, as near as possible to the French frontier. I have been in the museums and among the mountains. I have often thought of you, dear poet, in presence of the grandeur of nature and the eternity of art. Nature and art are yours; you have the double lyre.

Yes, dear Banville, you are one of the fountain-heads of poetry in our time; and that is a glory, for never has a great epoch had a more lofty poetry. In that firmament, which is often dark but always profound, you will rank among the stars of the first magnitude. You are an Aldebaran of art.

LXX.

To GEORGE SAND.

HAUTEVILLE HOUSE, 28*th November*, 1865.

You have just written me an admirable letter in the *Avenir national*. This article repays me for my book.[1] You are one of the great minds of France and of the world, and, what is the most beautiful thing in existence, a mind made up of heart. It is the heart, the large heart, which speaks in all that you utter, *urbi et orbi*. Having every tenderness, you have the right to promulgate every truth. There is something sublime and touching in witnessing the reappearance, in our century of doubt and strife, of the priestess in the imposing figure of George Sand. At their best, your ideas are heroic, because they are inspired by goodness. Hence your power. What you say of life, of death, of the grave, of the great gamut of souls on the lyre of the infinite, of the never-ending ascents, of the radiant transfigurations, — all this, which you bring before our eyes and into our thoughts, is true and pure, courageous to say, necessary to hear. A few minds, in our day, obtain notoriety by means of negation; affirmation is left to the great souls. You have the right to the Yes. Use it. Use it for yourself and for all. God has one proof among men, — genius. You exist, therefore He exists. I look on a profession of affirmation as a service rendered to the human race, and when it is written by you, it has a double light, glory added to truth. You are sad, O consoler! That enhances your greatness. Permit me to tell you that I am deeply moved.

[1] *Les chansons des rues et des bois.*

LXXI.

To PAUL DE SAINT-VICTOR.

HAUTEVILLE HOUSE, 10*th December*, 1865.

Solitude would be irksome without communion with great minds. I seek them in the past, and they reply to me; I call them in the present, and they reply to me there too. My books are the letters which I write to them. You have just acknowledged receipt of *Les chansons des rues et des bois.*

You have read this book, and you speak of it in grand terms. You have the gift of defining art in a line and of writing a poem in a page. Your criticism creates a picture, and there is a philosophy in your eloquence. This is the rule, however; there is no exception to it; splendor implies profundity.

This law is found in nature as well as in art. It breaks forth in the sun and is reflected in Homer. In my life on this rock amid the mist and the storm, my mind has gradually become detached from everything except the great manifestations of the conscience and the intellect. I have never indulged in hatred, and I am no longer moved by anger. I look only on the bright side of human nature; I grow wrathful only against absolute evil, pitying those who do it or think it. I have a profound faith in progress. Eclipses are intervals of obscuration, and how can I doubt of the return of liberty when each day that I wake I witness the return of light?

You, in this age which is too much inclined toward matter, are a dispenser of the ideal. You render us the immense service of making us understand the soul of the universe, demonstrated by the masterpieces of art as well as by the marvels of the creation. You are one of the luminaries of the true and the beautiful. Every time that my name drops from your pen, I fancy that I hear a rustle of glory.

LXXII.

To THE GONFALONIERE OF FLORENCE.

HAUTEVILLE HOUSE, 1st *February*, 1866.

SIR, — To receive from the Gonfaloniere of Florence, in the name of Italy, the jubilee medal of Dante, is an immense honor, and I am deeply touched by it. In your eyes my name is synonymous with France, and you say as much in grand terms. Yes, in me, as in all Frenchmen, there is something of the spirit of France, and this spirit of France is in favor of enlightenment, progress, peace, and liberty, and this spirit of France desires the greatness of all peoples, and this spirit of France has a sister in the spirit of Italy.

LXXIII.

To MME. RATTAZZI.

HAUTEVILLE HOUSE, 24th *February*, 1866.

Alas! madam, I appeal to your noble and charming heart and to your generous mind: after the crime committed against Italy at Mentana, not by France, but by the odious French government, I can only raise my voice in Italy to demand Rome and hail the republic. You will understand me, and you will approve of what I do.

VICTOR HUGO.

LXXIV.

To HENRI DE PÈNE, *Manager of the Gaulois.*

HAUTEVILLE HOUSE, 27*th February*, 1866.

MY HONORABLE AND DEAR OLD FRIEND, — I am much touched by your excellent letter. It is a pleasure to me to renew our friendly relations of former days. Your offers are the most splendid that have ever been made to a writer. I acknowledge your magnificence; but artistic considerations are paramount in my eyes, and even the half a million of francs which you offer me cannot overcome my scruples as an artist. I am convinced that *Les travailleurs de la mer* cannot be cut up into feuilletons. This mode of publication, excellent in itself and one which I am far from condemning, may perhaps suit *Quatrevingt-treize*, the book at which I am working just now.

Your letter and telegram reached me only yesterday. Our dear mutual friend Paul Meurice will explain to you the isolation of Guernsey. I live a retired, serious life here.

You will understand my reasons for declining your superb and handsomely made offers, and you will thank me for them. They spring entirely from my conscience. It is the latter which, however much I may regret it, forces me to turn my eyes away modestly from the half million. *Les travailleurs de la mer* is to appear in book form. When it is published, I am sure you will agree with me.

My warmest thanks for your cordial proposal. Allow me to put something of the future in the greeting which I send you.

LXXV.

To PAUL DE SAINT-VICTOR.

HAUTEVILLE HOUSE, *4th April*, 1866.

It would be worth while writing a book simply to get an article[1] from you. O brother of my mind, I greet you and I thank you. When the building is finished, it is you who plant the banner of light on the summit. You add one creation to another; you are the great interpreter; you write the poem on the poem, the answer to the Sphinx, the cry from the great deep. This grand criticism of yours is also a great philosophy; it flashes across our age like a trail of light through the darkness. You are one of the rescuers of the ideal. This distinction will attach to your name.

What escapes from the sea does not escape from woman; that is the subject of the book, and how you have understood it! And how you make others understand it! To be loved, Gilliatt does everything, Ebenezer nothing, and Ebenezer is the one who is loved. Ebenezer has spiritual and physical beauty, and with this twofold prestige, he has only to appear in order to triumph. Gilliatt too has this double beauty, but overlaid with the mask of frightful labor. His very greatness causes his defeat.

I am indulging in a conversation with you. I have just read your article, and it seems to me like a dialogue begun. When shall I see you? When will it be my lot to press the hand which has written so many superb and profound things, and which makes a masterpiece of criticism!

[1] Saint-Victor's article on *Les travailleurs de la mer*.

Bear in mind that you are one of the props of the solitary poet. A page written by you is like a cordial. Between you and me there is a sort of mysterious intercourse of the soul. You say to me: Courage! and I say to you: Thanks!

I seem to see my two poles marked out by you in your two articles on *Les chansons des rues et des bois* and *Les travailleurs de la mer*. Nothing escapes your powerful mind. You illumine the whole length and breadth of a work, and your star, after having lighted up the summit, reappears in the depths below.

LXXVI.
To LOUIS BOULANGER.

HAUTEVILLE HOUSE, *9th April,* 1866.

I am not absent, dear Louis, since I still keep my place in your heart.

Your letter charms and moves me; there is a flavor of our youth in it. You still keep that youth. A little child should have a young father, and your child is six years old. This dawning life blends sweetly with your own, and you have the radiance of it. Be happy. I constantly have before me, in my poor exile's abode, several powerful and striking works signed *Louis Boulanger*. I look at them and I meditate. Where are the roses of last year? You are still my beloved painter, the companion that I miss, one of those sweet brothers of the beginning, still more precious and more dear at the end.

LXXVII.

To MARC FOURNIER.

HAUTEVILLE HOUSE, 18*th April*, 1866.

MY DEAR COLLEAGUE, — I am touched by your obliging proposal. I recognize in it the talented writer as well as the artist-manager. I hasten to reply to you. To enable the drama[1] which I have written this winter to be acted, a state of liberty would be necessary which in France is granted to no one, and to me least of all. I am therefore compelled to put it off. The drama, however, is written for the stage, and entirely adapted for scenic effect. But, while quite playable from an artistic point of view, it is less so from the point of view of the censure. I prefer to wait, and my play will appear when liberty returns.

If, at that time, you are still good enough to remember me, we shall be able to resume this interrupted negotiation. The Porte-Saint-Martin theatre, which you so kindly call " my theatre," is dear to me, and there is no stage on which I should be more glad to reappear.

Accept, my dear and worthy colleague, with the expression of my *present* regret, the assurance of my warm regard.

LXXVIII.

To M. CUVILLIER-FLEURY.

HAUTEVILLE HOUSE, 30*th April*, 1866.

MY DEAR COLLEAGUE, — I feel, in every way, so utterly absent from the Academy that I cannot but be

---

[1] *Torquemada.*

touched whenever one of my colleagues is kind enough to make believe that I still belong to it. Exile has created the Academician *in partibus;* I am that Academician. But exile has not been able to rob me of my old memories and my old friendships. You know, my dear and worthy colleague, the place which you have in them.

There are, and I regret it, many points of disagreement between us; but we are agreed in this, that we both have conscience for our guide and liberty for our goal.

Conscience, liberty; all the dignity of life resides in those two words. We can, therefore, in the Academy and everywhere else, exchange a cordial shake of the hand.

LXXIX.

To M. LACAUSSADE.

HAUTEVILLE HOUSE, 30*th May*, 1866.

I knew and highly appreciated the poet in you; you now reveal to me the critic. One is worthy of the other. One feels that you are familiar with high art. I have just read your fine and thoughtful article on my lyric poetry. I am charmed, touched, and at times moved to delight, by the lofty, philosophical, and artistic qualities you display in these few pages.

You possess the two qualities without which no mind is complete, — that is to say, sympathy with your age and taste for all time; you understand the nineteenth century and you understand the ideal. Hence your power as a critic and your penetration as an artist.

Taste is much talked about in these days, and those

who talk the most about it are the people who have the least of it; they are engrossed in a local transitory taste, — French taste in the seventeenth century, — and they cannot appreciate what I have just called taste for all time.

Thus, in the name of Boileau they polish Horace, and in the name of Racine they deny Æschylus. To bring literature back from this spurious taste to the genuine taste, which embraces Aristophanes and Shakespeare, Dante and Molière, is the function of a mind such as yours. Function is equivalent to mission, and mission means the same as duty.

Continue your great work on the lines of the ideal. I thank you for myself, and I applaud you for all.

LXXX.

To MICHELET.

HAUTEVILLE HOUSE, 27*th May*, [1866].

. . . Your *Louis XV.* is one of your finest works. This king was rotting in his grave. You appeared on the scene as the resuscitator. You said to the corpse: Stand up! and you put within it its horrible soul. Now it moves, and it makes one shudder. And along with the reign, you have portrayed the age, — the one petty, the other great. The miasma of the past and the breath of the future are in your book; hence its warning and its encouragement, hence its lesson.

I thank you; I am only a witness of the nineteenth century. I will say this for myself, that I understand all the works of this great age, in which your place is such an exalted one. The sympathy which I feel for my time, and for the men of my time, constitutes all my pride and almost all my joy. Dear historian, dear philosopher, I press your hand, and I hail your luminous spirit.

LXXXI.
To Théodore de Banville.

BRUSSELS, 17th July, [1866].

I have just read *Gringoire*. You have written an exquisite work, intensely sad and intensely gay, like all true comedy. It is the sob of the poet mingling with the laugh of the philosopher. It is human destiny emphasized by ideal art. Your Louis XI. makes one shudder and smile; and what a charming figure of a woman between that spectre, the king, and that shadow, the poet! Your two ballads are beautiful and touching. I thank you, dear poet, for all the services which you render to the ideal. Go on giving me the pleasure of seeing you succeed. Thanks for my name side by side with yours.

LXXXII.
To the Same.

BRUSSELS, 8th August, [1866].

Oh, my dear poet, what beautiful things, and what charming things! Not a page but sparkles; not a word which does not sing and think, for to sing is to think. The Hymn is the Word. I have it, your book, this *living water, so dear to the heart of the wretched.* I drink of it, for I have suffered, and my mouth is dry. I am thirsty. Honor to you, poets, — *irrigui fontes!*

You yourself are one of the purest and most exquisite of these springs; your drops of water are pearls, and your pearls are tears, and your tears are my joy. Of such stuff is the poet. It is with his grief that he consoles. One touches one's wound and is healed. The grand poetry of the nineteenth century, daughter of the Revolution and of eternal liberty, encircles your head with one of its finest wreaths.

I embrace you, O sweet poet of poets, O ideal exile, friend of the Dantes and the Homers. You have *every fault* of the swan; you sing as he does, but you will not die.

LXXXIII.

To GEORGE SAND.

BRUSSELS, 14*th August,* 1866.

The echo of your fame still reaches me, although having become a chronic recluse (which results in a sort of deafness), I know nothing of what is going on. The idea of your story, *Un Don Juan de village,* is a lofty and profound one, like all that comes from your great mind. The unchangeableness of the perennial essence of human nature; the heart everywhere the same; the corruption of the town accentuated by the roughness of the country; vice growing in the fields as well as on the pavement; a peasant Don Juan,— all this bears the stamp of that great truth which is also great originality. And this vice tamed by love, this tiger on the back of which leaps the winged child, gentlest and strongest of beast-tamers, here again is greatness instinct with charm, greatness worthy of you.

I offer you my humble tribute of admiration.

LXXXIV.
To François Coppée.

CHAUDFONTAINE, *29th August*, [1866].

MY YOUNG AND CHARMING FELLOW-POET,—I have just arrived from Zealand, and your letter reaches me at Chaudfontaine. Yes, yes, yes; I wish to see you, you and your two excellent holiday companions. To press the hand of three poets, to commune with three *esprits*, is for me, an old recluse, a valuable opportunity, and I do not want to miss it. Only I shall not be at Brussels till the 15th.

We shall talk of you, of your fine book *Le reliquaire*, of art, of the ideal, of all that we desire, of all that we love. We shall mingle mind with mind, and your youth will bring me joy, and my old age will invite you to calm.

You will all three come, will you not, and dine with me at Brussels on the 15th?

LXXXV.
To MME. CHENAY.[1]

CHAUDFONTAINE, *3d September*, [1866].

We received your letters safely, dear Julie. Just now my wife can neither read nor write, but we are around her, and we do duty for her eyes. I brought her here because the country is a sort of green curtain. The summer, a furnace everywhere, is a vapor-bath here. One is not roasted; one is melted. It is a milder process. This steamy warmth and cool shade suit my wife. She has a whole forest for a screen.

---
[1] Mme. Victor Hugo's sister.

We shall be in Brussels about the 10th of September, and, if the equinox does not object too strongly, I hope to be in Guernsey by the end of September, if not earlier. It is high time for me to set to work again. We are all well here. As for me, my nightly spasms have been troubling me a little again, but I do not mention them to my family, as it would make them anxious, and there is no cause for anxiety. A little timely friction makes the symptoms disappear. I send you love from all who are mentioned in your letters, plus a pretty little smile from Master George. Victor is at Spa. I kiss you on both your cheeks, dear Julie.

LXXXVI.
To Paul de Saint-Victor.

Hauteville House, *20th January*, 1867.

What a happy thought to put these articles together in one volume! Splendid articles, grand volume, handful of stars! Your brilliant mind gives out an illumination. I thank you for this brightness. There is need of it; the night is upon us.

But, as you know, I am one of those who are not troubled by the night. I am sure of the morrow; in truth, I do not believe in the night nor in death. I believe only in the dawn.

I often wander along my paths by the seashore, pensive, thinking of France, contemplating the horizon without and the ideal within me. I sometimes take a book. I have my breviaries. You have just given me one.

The occasional mention of my name by your noble pen gives me the illusion of glory. Old and solitary,

I open my hands before the fire of your thought and warm myself at your luminous mind.

Tuus ex imo.

LXXXVII.
To Mme. Octave Giraud.

1867.

Madam, — You ask me, in terms which touch me deeply, to help you with your reminiscences of your husband. I can and I ought to do so. I am anxious to give the testimony which you demand from me. Yet it may be objected that I have never spoken to M. Octave Giraud, or had his manuscript in my hands. That is true, I never saw the man, but I know the mind; I never read the book, but I know the idea.

Besides, this idea, to a certain extent, comes from me. One day M. Giraud did me the honor to consult me. He had sent me some of his writings; I was aware of his knowledge, his intelligence, his travels, his studies in the Antilles, his fine poetic gift, his value as a writer, his significance as a philosopher. He said to me: What ought I to do? I replied: *Write the history of the black race.*

The black race, — what a subject! Till now the white man only has spoken. The white man is the master; the time has come for allowing the slave to speak. The white man is the tormentor; the time has come for hearing the victim. From the earliest ages, on this globe which is still so full of darkness, two faces confront each other and look dismally at each other, the white and the black face. One represents civilization, the other barbarism, — barbarism in two forms: willful barbarism, *i. e.*, savagery, and barbarism under compulsion, *i. e.*, slavery. One of these calamities comes from nature, the other from civilization. And here, let us proclaim it and denounce it, is the crime of the white man.

For six thousand years Cain has held the field. The black man is subjected to frightful violence at the hands of his brother. He suffers that long martyrdom called servitude. He is killed in his intelligence, in his will, in his soul. The human form which drags a chain is but a semblance. The slave may live, but the man is dead. What remains, what survives, is the brute, a beast of burden as long as it obeys, a wild beast when it revolts.

The whole history of the white man, the only one which has existed hitherto, is an enormous mass of facts, of doings, of struggles, of advances, of catastrophes, of revolutions, of movements in every direction, of which the black man is the melancholy caryatid. Slavery is the monstrous fact in history.

Underneath our civilization, such as it is, with its magnificent deformities, its splendors, its trophies, its triumphs, its flourishes of trumpets, its rejoicings, a cry is heard. This cry rises from under our fêtes. We hear it through the marble of our temples and palaces. This cry is slavery. What a mission and what a task, to write the history of this cry!

The proletariate in Europe, quite a different and no less vast a question, is connected by some of its ramifications with slavery. But the human problem in Europe is complicated by the social question, which imparts to it a tremendous originality. It is the tragic new-born child of modern fatality. In Africa, in Asia, in America, the situation, though not less heart-rending, is more simple. Color stamps its unity on the outcast and on the vanquished. The great funereal type is the negro. The slave has the same countenance as the darkness.

To dispel this fatal darkness is the supreme effort of civilization. We are on the brink of this victory. America is well-nigh delivered from slavery. I have said it more than once, — and I like to indulge in the hopeful thought, — the time is drawing near when man will be free. What are two colors under the same sun ! what are two different shades, if on the pale face and on the dark face there is the same morning light, — fraternity !

Beneath all exteriors the soul is white.

The resurrection of the slave in liberty ! deliverance ! reconciliation of Cain and Abel !

That is the history to be written. The Black Race is the title; the subject is slavery.

M. Giraud was worthy of this great undertaking. To thoroughly sift and exhaustively scrutinize the material it was necessary to have studied the slave and slavery on the spot. M. Giraud had a considerable advantage; he had seen with his eyes. The slave had said to him : *Vide pedes, vide manus.* Slavery is the wound in the side of humanity. M. Giraud has put his finger in that wound.

He took this book in hand; he almost completed it. A short respite from death, and he would have finished it. How melancholy are these interruptions !

Such as it is, his work is considerable. The fragments which have been published in the newspapers, and which are known to all, have placed the history and the writer on a high pedestal. This poignant story has the pathetic interest of a drama. There is no more painful struggle, no more tragic contest. The whole question at issue between the white man and the black man is there. M. Giraud gives it to us with the corroborating proofs. It is the brief against slavery made up and almost completed. Now let us decide the case. The sentence has been pronounced, we may say, by the conscience of the world, and slavery is condemned, and slavery is dead.

LXXXVIII.

To ALBERT CAISE.[1]

HAUTEVILLE HOUSE, 20*th March*, 1867.

... The point raised by the anonymous writer to whom you refer admits of the simplest explanation. These matters are of very slight importance, but what is certain is that you are right, and that the anonymous writer is not wrong.

The relationship to the Bishop of Ptolemais is a tradition in my family. I never knew more than what my father told me about it. M. Buzy, formerly a notary at Epinal, sent me some documents of his own accord, which are among my papers.

Personally I do not attach any importance to genealogical questions. The man is what he is; his value is what he has done. Beyond this, all that is added to or taken from him is nothing. Hence my absolute contempt for genealogies.

---

[1] M. Albert Caise had published a genealogy of Victor Hugo, in which he assigned him the arms of the Hugos of Lorraine. An anonymous writer discussed this in the *Figaro*, asking where Hugo, Bishop of Ptolemais, was to be placed in the genealogy.

The Hugos from whom I am descended are, I believe, a younger and possibly illegitimate branch, which had come down in the world through poverty and misery. A Hugo was a breaker-up of boats on the Moselle. Mme. de Graffigny (Françoise Hugo, wife of the chamberlain of Lorraine) addressed him as "my cousin." The "wise and witty anonymous writer" is right; there were a shoemaker and a bishop, beggars and prelates, in my family. This is more or less the case with everybody. There are very curious instances of it in the Channel Islands (see *Les travailleurs de la mer*, — Tangrouille).

In other words, I am not a Tangroville, I am a Tangrouille. I have no objection. If I could choose my forbears, I would rather have a hard-working cobbler for an ancestor than a lazy king.

LXXXIX.
To GEORGE SAND.[1]

HAUTEVILLE HOUSE, 21*st April*, [1867].

Yes, I suffer; yes, I hope. Your child has been restored to you, mine will return; I believe it, I know it. Your tender and lofty letter would give me faith, if I did not possess it. O great soul, I take refuge in you. The words which fall from your pinnacle of glory are sweet as light itself.

Thanks.

XC.
To THE COMMITTEE FOR ERECTING A MONUMENT TO MICKIEWICZ.

HAUTEVILLE HOUSE, GUERNSEY, 17*th May*, 1867.

I am asked to say a few words over this illustrious grave. . . .

---
[1] After the death of Charles Hugo's first child.

To speak of Mickiewicz is to speak of all that is beautiful, just, and true; it is to speak of the right of which he was the champion, of the duty of which he was the hero, of the liberty of which he was the apostle, of the deliverance of which he is the forerunner.

Mickiewicz evoked all the ancient virtues which have in them a rejuvenating power; he was a priest of the ideal; his art is the great art; his poetry is instinct with the mighty breath of the sacred forests. And he understood humanity as well as nature; through his hymn to the infinite runs the holy throb of revolution. Banished, proscribed, vanquished, he proudly flung to the four corners of the earth the lofty claims of the fatherland. The reveille of peoples is the genius which sounds it; of old it was the prophet, now it is the poet; and Mickiewicz is one of the clarions of the future.

There is life in such a grave.

Immortality is in the poet, resurrection is in the citizen.

One day the United Peoples of Europe will say to Poland: Arise! and his great soul will come forth from this tomb.

Yes, Poland, that sublime spirit, lies there with the poet. Hail to Mickiewicz! Hail to the noble sleeper who will awake! He hears me, I know it, and he understands me. He and I are two absent ones. If, in my isolation and in my gloom, I have no crown to bestow in the name of glory, I have the right to fraternize with a spirit in the name of misfortune. I am not the voice of France, but I am the cry of exile.

XCI.

To CHAMPFLEURY.

BRUSSELS, 5*th August*, 1867.

MY DEAR COLLEAGUE, — Wanderers and absentees miss a great deal. Living in Guernsey, traveling to Brussels, crossing the sea twice, all this accounts for my not reading your *Belle Paule*, which was published in May, until July.

I come to the point at once. I like the book. I like it because it is true and profound, because it despises petty artifices, because it goes straight to the great goal of art, the creation of types by means of observation and intuition, because it is written in a charming style, because it is dedicated to me and composed for all, an extension which doubles the honor of the dedication. Yes, for all. A day will come when, thanks to the universal character of education, thanks to the advent of broad daylight in men's minds, works of art will be essentially popular. The people has at bottom a refined taste. It likes poets, it demands the ideal, it prefers a heavenly luminary to a Chinese lantern. Writers of your stamp have a lofty function to discharge towards it. Vulgar is not the same as popular. And not being vulgar is a reason for being popular. There is a fine apprehension and a stern will in the people. That is also the basis of the artist. So continue. Success supplies the inducement, talent creates the obligation.

Your story is life and truth from one end to the other. It is what you have observed, what you have seen; it is real; at the same time, nature is everywhere set off by art; hence, a book!

XCII.

To M. CHASSAGNAC, *Grand Commander of the Rite Ecossais in Louisiana.*

BRUSSELS, 16*th August,* 1867.

You are right, dear sir; although not a Freemason in name, I am one in heart. My Freemasonry is loftier than yours, it is humanity.

You wish, in your nobility of mind and heart, to admit black men into your ranks, and you are right; *I* wish for the peaceful transformation of the prince into the man, and of the king into the citizen. Time is required for this. Be it so; God has no lack of it.

In the mean while, not being able to associate with the princes whom you admit, I am prohibited from joining you. But I appreciate your lofty aim and your splendid fraternity, symbol of the great fraternity of the future.

I thank you for having informed me of the great and serious step in advance which you have just taken; the admission of black men among you is the beginning of equality, which the exclusion of princes will complete.

XCIII.

To THE REVOLUTIONARY COMMITTEE OF PORTO RICO.

HAUTEVILLE HOUSE, 24*th November,* 1867.

The Republic of Porto Rico has fought bravely for its liberty. The revolutionary committee acquaints me of this, and I thank it for doing so. Spain turned out of America! that is the great aim; that is the great duty for Americans. Cuba free like St. Domingo. I applaud all these great efforts.

The liberty of the world is made up of the liberty of each people.

XCIV.

To ALFRED SIRVEN.[1]

HAUTEVILLE HOUSE, 8*th December*, 1867.

Of all prisons, the one which I know the best is exile. I have been turning in that cage for nearly sixteen years.

I know Sainte-Pélagie from the outside only. As a child, I played in the Jardin des Plantes. I used to go to the top of the maze, and I saw a large flat roof, on which was a sentry-box, and a soldier strolling up and down, with a gun in his hand. My mother said to me: "It is a prison!"

A prison can be very large. A flat thing, on which a soldier walks about, describes the Europe of to-day.

Later on, I heard about the interior of Sainte-Pélagie from two old friends of mine, Béranger and Lamennais. Béranger wrote to me shortly before his death: "I began with imprisonment, and you end with exile." And I replied to him: "All is for the best! Let us hope! The future is a dawn."

XCV.

To THÉODORE DE BANVILLE.

HAUTEVILLE HOUSE, 20*th December*, [1867].

You are an exquisite poet and a charming friend. Do not be afraid, the variations of the magnetic needle called *fashion* are meaningless; they govern only the Scribe drama and Feuillet literature. Where you are, is taste; where you are, is art.

---

[1] In reply to a request for information about the prison of Sainte-Pélagie.

Your exquisite, your beautiful odes in the *Charivari* appeal to *La voix de Guernesey*. Here it is. You will find it in a separate envelope. My echo answers you: —

"Echo n'est plus un son qui dans l'art retentisse,
C'est une voix qui dit: Droit, Liberté, Justice."

I have corrected for you, in the copy which I am sending, a wrong rhyme, *ennemis, amis*, which is in Voltaire, which quite condemns it. This rhyme comes from a mistake of the copyist, who substituted an erased line for the right one. Give me absolution.

Who on earth could have told you that I never put the names of my friends in my verses? Some day you may find out the contrary to your cost. You may take this threat as a promise.

Is there no chance of your coming to see my ocean? Just now it is terrible, but sublime. If you are not afraid of its wrath, come and spend a month or two with me. You will have a poor lodging, but will be well taken care of.

XCVI.

To ALFRED ASSELINE.

HAUTEVILLE HOUSE, 22*d December*, 1867.

MY DEAR ALFRED, — I have received your charming letter, and have looked carefully in the pockets of the pair of trousers. Result, nothing! nothing! nothing! (Desmousseaux de Civré[1]). It is as empty as the noddle of an Academician. I am like Margaret of Savoy, a widow before the wedding. I am lamenting my loss.

It is probable that in packing the trousers they

---

[1] A deputy in the reign of Louis Philippe, who addressed Guizot as follows: "Qu'avez-vous fait? Rien! rien! rien!"

dropped the little case, which was in the fob. Do have a good search made.

But the case alone is not enough for me; we want your wife and you. Can't you manage to come to Guernsey for a time? Unfortunately I have no suitable apartment for Mme. Asseline, but a place at table morning and evening, *castaneæ molles,* this is what I offer you.

Give my respects to your wife into the bargain, and be jealous.

12 P. M. *Latest news.* — As I was about to close this letter the post arrived, and a little box with a stamp is brought me; it is the case! I open it and am lost in admiration. Nothing could be more charming. It is a perfect gem. It is historical and fanciful. Thanks, dear poet, for this pretty thing.

Very latest. — A lot of people in my house for the poor children's Christmas entertainment. A number of charming women. Your delightful case has been handed round. Universal admiration. Strange to say, it has not been stolen.

XCVII.

To FRANÇOIS COPPÉE.

HAUTEVILLE HOUSE, *5th January,* [1868].

Just as I was sending you my angry poetry, you were forwarding me your charming poetry. *La voix de Guernesey* met your sweet idyl of the soldier and the servant girl on the road. My lightning crossed your sunbeam.

Power of the poet! Here are the private soldier and the nursemaid transfigured. They will no longer be laughed at. What an elegy you have managed to extract from these hitherto grotesque figures. *Melancholia.* We always have to revert to the great allegorical bat of Albert Dürer. Melancholy is our background. Life is enacted in front; God is behind. Let us hope.

Will you forward the inclosed to M. Paul Verlaine, your friend and mine?

XCVIII.

To THÉOPHILE GAUTIER.

HAUTEVILLE HOUSE, 29*th April*, 1868.

DEAR THÉOPHILE, — I have just read your splendid article on *La légende des siècles.* I am more than touched by it; I am deeply moved. So sweet voices still reach me in my solitude. Our youthful attachment has become an old friendship. The great gulf between us does not prevent your glance from seeking mine and my hand from pressing yours. You give me one of your wreaths, you who have the right to all. As a poet, you are a spokesman of the ideal; as a critic, you are a spokesman of glory.

Why has a laurel grown on this spot? Because Petrarch once spoke there.

What was said of Petrarch will be said of you.

Where your criticism casts its seed, the laurel will spring up.

XCIX.
To Mme. Chenay.

BRUSSELS, 27th *August*, 7 A. M., [1868].

MY POOR JULIE,— Your sister is dead. This beloved creature has left us.

On the 24th she was in perfect health, she was driving about Brussels with us in excellent spirits. The day before yesterday, the 25th, she had an attack; yesterday, the 26th, Dr. Allix, who had been summoned by telegraph, arrived. There was a consultation of the doctors; in the evening, a little hope; this morning, at half past six, she passed away. I am broken-hearted. God will receive this gentle and lofty soul into light. She now has wings. *We* are in tears. I am overwhelmed with grief.

I send you my fond love, my dearest sister, as do all of us. Alas! your tears will flow as well as ours.

C.
To Auguste Vacquerie.

1st *September*, 1868.

You are admirable as you always are, and you have done everything well. Thank your family, which so many pleasing and painful points of contact have made mine as well. I have had five sleepless nights; my eyes are all sore. Meurice's exquisite letter has relieved them by making my tears flow. All that you mention shall be done. Glory will soon be yours; that will console me. I am deeply attached to you.

As soon as you have received this letter, go and press your lips to the three graves for me.

CI.

To PAUL MEURICE.

BRUSSELS, 1*st September*, [1868].

Meurice, my gentle and noble friend, I have read your touching farewell to the dear lost one, and my tears break forth afresh. They had stopped and were choking me.

You make me weep. Thanks.

CII.

To VICTOR PAVIE.

3*d September*, [1868].

I am broken-hearted; I feel that you still love me a little; I hear your voice as the voice of my past and of my youth, a sweet and solemn appeal. I am old. I shall soon go to join the great soul which has just departed.

CIII.

To THÉODORE DE BANVILLE.

3*d September*, [1868].

DEAR, GENTLE POET,— You know how to give fitting and lofty consolation. I suffer, and your message makes me feel that I am loved, and that I still live.

CIV.

To G. MARGIN, *Editor of the Phare de la Loire.*

HAUTEVILLE HOUSE, 18*th November*, 1868.

MY DEAR COLLEAGUE,— Do you really want the information? Here is the truth about my supposed income of 78,000 francs. I am quite ready to talk about my affairs to a friend like you.

After all the losses entailed by exile, the following was my position at the end of August last, when the accounts to which your correspondent refers were sent in. I have : —

	Francs.
1stly in Belgium, 300 shares in the National Bank, fluctuating income, at most	35,000
2dly in England, I shall have next April (investment of proceeds of my recent works) in English consols, 425,000 francs, income	12,500
3dly in France, allowance from the Institute . . .	1,000
4thly Hauteville House; lodging, no income; I pay rent at Brussels.	
	48,500
In consequence of family arrangements which have had to be made I have to pay out of these 48,500 a yearly sum of	29,500
In addition to this I spend every year, on various charitable objects, especially on a small charitable institution for children which I have started, about (minimum)	7,000
	36,500

which, subtracted from the 48,500, leave me an income of my own of 12,000 francs; as I have children, I consider myself entitled to a life interest only.

All this is confidential and does not require publicity, for nothing in this little statement can interest the public. But I am anxious to give information to a high-minded and sympathetic man like you; when opportunity offers, you will remember this letter, and when you see me calumniated, you will know the truth. That is enough for me. In public I prefer silence on such matters.

One word more. Your correspondent is right if he meant that I *had* an income of 78,000 francs (and even more) out of the receipts from my plays; this is perfectly true, only my plays are not acted now. All this between ourselves.

CV.

To FRANÇOIS MORAND, *Judge at Boulogne-sur-Mer.*

HAUTEVILLE HOUSE, 22d *November*, 1868.

I answer your question, dear sir, for you are witty, learned, and charming (I refer here to literature only). No, I did not know *L'Arlequin* of Le Sage, and I have been delighted to make acquaintance with it through you. The resemblances which you point out to me are very real. The result for me is the inward satisfaction, because my conscience confirms it, of having fortuitously used the same expressions as the great writer who created *Gil Blas*.

May I tell you of another coincidence of which I was still more proud? It was in 1823. Lamennais, who had been my confessor (which of us two *perverted* the other?), came to see me one morning. I was writing some lines which I had just composed. Lamennais looked over my shoulder and read the following:

> "Ephémère histrion qui sait son rôle à peine,
> Chaque homme ivre d'audace ou palpitant d'effroi,
> Sous le sayon du pâtre ou la robe du roi,
> Vient passer, à son tour, son heure sur la scène."

"Hullo!" he said, "do you know English?" I replied: "No" (I do not know English even now). And I added: "Why?" "Because," replied Lamennais, "you have just written a line of Shakespeare."

"Bah!" "Have you read Shakespeare?" "No, I don't want to read Le Tourneur." "Well," said Lamennais (my ex-confessor, who knew that I was speaking the truth), "you are both authors of the line. You have hit on the same idea as Shakespeare." And he quoted a line from *Macbeth*, with the same comparison as mine and almost the same words: *each man in turn spends his hour upon the stage.*[1]

Now decide, my dear judge.

A word about a more serious matter in your communication.

I had as little to do with M. Granier de Cassagnac's article (1833) on Alexandre Dumas as yourself. Read the declaration of M. Bertin the elder, in the *Journal des Débats*. Read the declaration of M. Granier de Cassagnac, which he would confirm even to-day, I am sure, although we are as wide apart as the poles.

Do you want my word of honor about this? I give it to you. If you knew me well, you would not need it.

And I press your hand, and I thank you for having made me acquainted with Le Sage's *Sérendib* and *L'Arlequin*. In politics, I would take exception to you; but in literary matters I accept you, my most amiable judge, my courteous colleague.

[1] "Life's but a walking shadow; a poor player,
That struts and frets his hour upon the stage."

CVI.

To M. d'Alton-Shée.

Hauteville House, 8*th December*, 1868.

I look on your Memoirs, my dear d'Alton, as messages from your noble mind. Once more thanks, and once more bravo to these hearty and sturdy pages.

On the fortifications of Paris my view is as follows: *I would not have built them, but I would not destroy them.* They should not be pulled down till the morrow of the day when Europe will be proclaimed a republic in its parliament, sitting in the meeting-place of the Federation of Paris. Then all barriers will fall and all hearts will open. You, my dear d'Alton, will belong to that parliament; I, too, perhaps, — if I am not dead.

I have a long-standing and deep sympathy with you. You are a citizen with a gentleman's pride and a nobleman's dignity. Your mind is lofty because it is free. You are fraternal with all, and in your old age, if need be, paternal. You commend yourself to my exile. You and I are the only two republican peers. I feel as if you were a sort of brother to me. I am your senior in age only; for you had understood and wished for the Republic before me. My belated logic reached it some time after yours. Armand Carrel had a good deal to do with this delay. If it were worth while to make a reproach out of it, the responsibility would lie with him.

I reply to your question. I heard of my appointment to the peerage on *the 16th of April,* 1845. Twenty years before, to a day, I had heard, almost in the same way, that I was decorated. I note this only because Lamartine and I were made members of the Legion of Honor on the same day (16th of April, 1825), no one else being appointed at the time.

CVII.

To Jules Claretie.[1]

31st December, 1868.

. . . It is *el Puente de los Contrabandistas*. I saw it in the Pyrenees, when I was a child. The Smugglers' Bridge was a terrible thing. It was used as a bridge by smugglers and as a gallows by justice. They were hung to the beams. That did not prevent them from continuing to pass over it. The bridge was also described as follows : —

ON MARCHE DESSUS,
ON DANSE DESSOUS.

I quoted, in the *Dernier jour d'un condamné*, the melancholy lines : —

"Je lui ferai donner la danse
Où il n'y a pas de plancher."

This dismal dance is what I am sending you. Forgive me. It is repulsive, but useful. The executioners must have their work brought under their noses. So let us show up the horrors of the past.

The present is not much more attractive. But what a Morrow you will have, you who are young ! *I* shall be dead.

[1] Sending him a drawing.

CVIII.

To Mme. Rattazzi.

1st January, 1869.

What can I say? I am dazzled, intoxicated, overwhelmed. Your tender friendship gives me a glimpse of paradise, and I cannot enter it; I am bound and sentenced by my own line.

"Revenir sur ses pas à la porte du ciel!"

I wrote that and I am under its orders. This winter they thought I was very ill; the doctors told me that I must make a rapid journey across France and go to Nice. I replied: I have made an oath, I cannot put foot in France; I would sooner die first! But it is much easier to die than to resist you. When I think that she is there, facing me, she who unites all, she who combines beauty, grace, courage, commanding and bewitching intelligence, brilliant acquirements, deep poetry, and that she says to me: Come! and in such affecting and enchanting terms! — oh! not to obey, not to come, not to hasten to the spot, not to trample on the frontier, were it red-hot iron, and on the oath, were it writ in brass, do you know, madam, that that is a superhuman effort, and that I am almost prostrated by it! What! it is you who send me this flower! it is you who have written these lines! they were composed by you, they are destined for me, on your lips plays that angelic smile in which I fancy I see the birth of a star. That heavenly smile will welcome me. And I stay where I am! Alas! try to fathom the depth of this regret. What a stern thing sometimes is duty! I wrote this: —

"Et s'il n'en reste qu'un, je serai celui-là !"

France is closed to me, and France, when you are not there, is the fatherland, and when you are there, is paradise.

You write to me also these words, which issue from your heart like a ray of light: "I shall not feel quite settled in Paris, and glad to be there, until *you* are there, too. What nice talks we shall have! And how softly and poetically the time will glide by." I read these adorable lines, these still more adorable plans, over and over again, and my hand trembles. Does your youth reflect on my years? Am I Æschylus, to be the chosen friend, as you say, in spite of my gray hairs, of queen Rhodope, of the dazzling Rhodope, who was alike the genius and the sovereign of Acragas, and who was of the blood of Zeus as you are of the blood of Napoleon? She preferred the aged Æschylus, who, like her, was a genius, to the young Hieron, who was a sovereign like her. But I, am I Æschylus, and would it not be better that you should not see me again?

This letter which I am writing distresses me deeply, but I feel that it will not vex you, that it will even please you. I know your lofty character too well to doubt for a moment of your approval of my painful sacrifice. A bitter sacrifice! but you are capable of understanding as well as of inspiring every act of heroism, and I declare, I am a hero to-day, to-day for the first time. Resist you, great Heavens! all that I have done hitherto is as nothing compared with what I am doing now; but since you are my friend, since your regard has a place in my life, I ought to remain worthy of this celestial friendship.

To hide myself, to creep into France, even for the purpose of seeing you, of obeying you, to crouch uneasily under the eye of the police, to lower myself in the sight of your cousin and your persecutor, even for the sake of basking once more in your sunlight, of entering into your heaven, — this I must not do. You are my best friend, my brave friend, you are attached to me, therefore you approve my decision.

I keep your letter indelibly engraven on my heart. I was away when it arrived, and I have just found it on my return, and I write to you in deep emotion, for I fancy that it is your angelic soul which has just exhaled from the flower to which I have pressed my lips.

CIX.
To M. COELLOPOULO.

12th January, [1869].

Your eloquent letter has touched me deeply. Yes, you are right in counting upon me as a writer and as a citizen. The little that I am and the little that I can do is at the service of your noble cause.

The cause of Crete is that of Greece, and the cause of Greece is that of Europe. These connections escape the notice of kings and are nevertheless the height of logic. Diplomacy is simply the stratagems of princes against the logic of God. But in the end God prevails. God and right are synonymous.

I am but a single voice, stubborn, but lost in the triumphal tumult of reigning iniquity. What matter! listened to or not, I shall go on. You tell me that Crete asks me for what Spain has asked of me. Alas! I can but utter a cry. For Crete I have already done so; I will do it again.

I belong to Greece as much as to France. I am ready to give my stanzas for Greece like Tyrtæus, and my blood like Byron. Your sacred country has my deepest love. I think of Athens as one thinks of the sun.

CX.

To FRANÇOIS COPPÉE.

HAUTEVILLE HOUSE, 30*th January*, 1869.

You send me your work, but public rumor had already told me of your success. It was more than an echo of rejoicing, it was an echo of glory. Paris has hailed you a poet. My dear and charming colleague, I have read your *Passant*. I am delighted. It is excellent versification, strong and tender thought, the total effect exquisite.

You have harmoniously brought the moon into the landscape and melancholy into the poem, — an atmosphere which makes the thinker meditate.

To write a work like this is admirable; to achieve such a success is perfect. Our generous youth has understood you. You are a priest of the true and great art; the rising generation applauds you, and I cry out to you, Thanks! and to them, Bravo!

CXI.

To MME. CESSIAT DE LAMARTINE.[1]

HAUTEVILLE HOUSE, 10*th March*, 1869.

Since the year 1821 I have been warmly attached to Lamartine. This friendship of fifty years now undergoes the momentary eclipse of death. I did not like, just at first, to intrude on your sorrow with my sym-

[1] On the death of Lamartine.

pathy; but at the present moment you will allow me, will you not, to communicate to you — to you who were connected with him by blood, who loved him and were loved by him — my profound grief. Every form of glory, from popularity to immortality, belongs to Lamartine, luminous poet, powerful and immortal orator. He seems dead to us, he is not really so. Lamartine has not ceased to give forth his light. Henceforth he shines with a twofold radiance: in our literature as a genius, and in the great unknown life as a star.

CXII.

To VICTORIEN SARDOU.

HAUTEVILLE HOUSE, 31*st March*, [1869].

MY DEAR COLLEAGUE, — You have written my son Charles a letter which touches and moves me. In the blaze of your dazzling success, you bestow a thought on a recluse, twice banished, yesterday exiled from France, to-day exiled from the stage. I thank you from the bottom of my heart.

Your triumphant work, *Patrie,* rekindles lofty sentiments and proud thoughts, and you, at any rate, are entitled to say to the spectators whose republicanism you have just reinvigorated: *Plaudite cives!*

CXIII.

To MME. CHENAY.

LONDON, *Sunday the* 23*d* [*May*, 1869].

MY DEAR LITTLE SISTER, — Your letters are as nice as yourself. I am a lazy old brute, which accounts for my not having duly replied to you. To-day I do better than this, I am on my way home. However, a strong southwesterly gale is blowing, and we shall not be able to land in Guernsey till the 26th (Wednesday).

You may prepare for that occasion the various triumphal arches you have in stock, the addresses, the keys of Hauteville on a massive golden salver, the profound obeisances of the cat and her kitten, and the Latin verses which I beg you to write in my honor.

I hope the wind will go down. The crossing from Ostend, very good for the first four hours, was awful at the end. I kiss you on your two nice cheeks.

CXIV.

To SWINBURNE.

HAUTEVILLE HOUSE, 14*th July*, [1869].
The great date.

DEAR AND CORDIAL POET, — I was deeply touched by your letter and your article.

You are right: you, Byron, and Shelley, three aristocrats, three republicans. And I, it is from aristocracy that I have risen to democracy, it is from the peerage that I have arrived at the Republic, as one passes from a river to the ocean. These are striking phenomena. Nothing is so significant as these victories of the truth.

Thanks, *ex imo corde,* for your splendid article on my book.[1] What lofty philosophy, what profound intuition you have! In the great critic, one feels the great poet.

VICTOR HUGO.

---

[1] *L'homme qui rit.*

CXV.

To L. HUGONNET.

BRUSSELS, 24*th August*, 1869.

I have been very slow, dear sir, in replying to you. It is not my fault. I live in a vortex, a strange thing for a recluse. No leisure. Not a moment to myself. But I was anxious to read your paper; it is excellent. Yes, you are right, France is for Africa what England is for Asia, a bad guardian. To teach barbarism the rudiments of civilization is the duty and the right of older peoples. This right and this duty are not better understood by the French government than by the English government. Hence your complaints, in which I join.

When the Republic returns, justice will return. The real light of France will shine in Africa. Let us hope. Let us wait. Let us struggle on.

You are a young and noble mind. Your generation, somewhat belated, will end by doing great things, in which you will share. I congratulate you beforehand. *I* shall be dead. I shall bequeath to you all my spirit.

CXVI.

To FRANÇOIS COPPÉE.

HAUTEVILLE HOUSE, 10*th January*, 1870.

MY YOUNG AND DEAR FELLOW-POET, — I have received, from you I believe, your fine poem *Les forgerons*. *Qua* philosopher and democrat, I am unable to accept the standpoint; but *qua* poet, I applaud, together with the delighted public, all these firm, vigorous, and pathetic lines.

Go on with your great successes; you will end, I hope, by turning altogether, like myself, towards the people. The truth lies in that direction.

As for beauty, you know where to find it.

CXVII.

To HENRI ROCHEFORT.

HAUTEVILLE HOUSE, 10*th February*, 1870.

I have written to you several times; I doubt whether my letters have reached you. I make this one small so that it may arrive at its destination. Being after the image of the Empire, it will pass unobserved, I hope.

You are now in prison; I congratulate the Revolution. Your popularity is as unbounded as your talent and your courage. All that you have foretold is coming to pass. Henceforth you are one of the forces of the future.

I am, as ever, your sincere friend, and I press your hand, dear prisoner, dear conqueror.

CXVIII.

To EDGAR QUINET.

26*th February*, 1870.

Old age is the age of adding up, for thoughts as well as for years, for the mind as well as for life. Only the total of years is overwhelming, the total of thoughts is sustaining. Hence the result that, while the body decays, the mind expands. There is a sort of dawn within it.

This mysterious rejuvenation, of which, like you, I am aware, this doubling of the moral and intellectual forces while the material force is sinking, this growth in decay, what a magnificent proof it is of the soul! The enfeebled cerebral matter gives forth a more vigorous thought. Of the two beings, the one organic, the other essential, which make up the man, the first crumbles away, the second breaks its bonds. The mind sees the grave and feels the spring. It creates up to the last moment — sublime promise of the great unknown life which it is about to enter. Its span augments. The process resembles an unfolding of the wings.

CXIX.

To Paul Verlaine.

Hauteville House, 16*th April*, 1870.

No one is a poet if he is not so in both kinds, which are Force and Grace. I have always fancied that this was the meaning of the twin peaks of Parnassus. You are capable, my young fellow-poet, of flitting from one summit to the other. After *Les fêtes galantes*, a charming book, you will give us *Les vaincus*, a sturdy book.

Your noble mind is full of promise. Emotion, tears, sympathy, this is the point which your young and lofty talent will reach, after so much admirable poetry. To be inspired is a fine thing; to be moved is great.

You know that I told you your fortune at Brussels and said that this would be your future. You are one of the first, one of the most attractive, one of the strongest, in the new sacred legion of poets which I hail and which I love, I the dreamy old dweller in the wilderness.

What a number of delicate and ingenious things in

that pretty little book, *Les fêtes galantes!* "These shells of the seashore!" What a gem the last line is! I send you my best wishes for success, and a cordial shake of the hand.

VICTOR HUGO.

CXX.

To M. D'ALTON-SHÉE.

HAUTEVILLE HOUSE, 2d August, 1870.

MY DEAR D'ALTON, — I quite agree with you. A solution must be found. At a given moment civilization, with revolution for its mouthpiece, must stop the combatants. I wish to see France have the Rhine, because it is necessary to form, both materially and intellectually, as strong a French group as possible, to make head against the German group in the parliament of the United States of Europe, and impose the French language on the European federation.

The United States of Europe speaking German would mean a delay of three hundred years. A delay, that is to say, a step backward. When I see you, I will develop this idea. But nothing through Bonaparte! nothing from this frightful war!

CXXI.

To PAUL MEURICE.

BRUSSELS, 19th August, 1870.

DEAR MEURICE, — I am sending you this telegram: "I am returning as a national guard of Paris. I shall arrive on the 21st of August." But I am told that you will not get it, so I write to you as well. Your letter arrived at Guernsey after I had left, and reached me here to-day at two o'clock. We went at once,

Charles and I, to the Foreign Office. I declared that I did not recognize the French Empire, that I submitted, by constraint and under compulsion, to the abusive formality of the passport, and I gave my name. Thereupon they sent for the minister, who was not at the office. His immediate substitute, with a rosette in his buttonhole, came instead, was very polite, and asked my leave to *begin by saluting the great poet of the century*. I replied with courtesy to the man of the world, and I repeated my protest with firmness to the official by calling on him to deliver me a passport.

He hesitated. I said: I wish to be nothing more in France than one of the national guard. He bowed. Charles said: And so do I. He promised us passports, but asked my permission not to send them till this evening. That is how matters stand.

You approve of what I have done, do you not? I want to return to France, to return to Paris, openly, simply, as a national guard, with my two sons at my side. I shall enroll myself in the district where I take up my abode, and I shall go to the ramparts with my rifle on my shoulder.

All this without prejudice to my duty in other respects. I want no share of power, but I want my full share of danger.

My gentle and intrepid friend, what happiness to do one's duty by your side!

CXXII.

To PAUL MEURICE.

BRUSSELS, 26*th August*, 1870.

DEAR MEURICE, — We are on the lookout; the refugees are conferring together; the situation, which was clear, is becoming obscure. No news from outside. The two marshals, MacMahon and Bazaine, jealous, perhaps, of one another, looking for and not finding each other, and MacMahon putting the emperor back into the saddle. As for the Prussians, hesitating advance, slow progress; fear of the trap laid for them; to sum up, nothing decisive as yet. In France, unsatisfactory symptoms; the Empress reappearing on the scene; the Right raising their heads; Baroche, Rouher, and Persigny back again; Trochu ridiculed by the Bonapartist papers, and losing prestige. Probable jealousy, too, in that quarter; Palikao hates Trochu. The Republican papers are not coming out again. A *coup d'état* is even talked of as probable.

It is evident that a decisive battle, victory or defeat, Jena or Rosbach, will clear the ground. France is entitled to victory; the Empire ought to fall. Which will God choose?

I shall not make up my mind until the situation clears. In case of a Rosbach, I shall go to Paris at once, for the danger may be great, and I feel that I belong alike to Europe and to Paris. To protect Paris with a living rampart will be the duty of all. In case of a Bonapartist victory and a *coup d'état*, I shall gather my family around me at Hauteville House; that is to say, that I offer you as well as Auguste hospitality there. In the mean while . . . we wait.

CXXIII.

To Paul Meurice.

Brussels, 1*st September*, 1870.

They tell me not to wear myself out; to keep myself for the decisive moment; but will this decisive moment come? Your noble, tender letter has just reached me, and moves me deeply. You end with a question. I cannot intrust my reply to the post, but Jules Claretie will give it you by word of mouth. He has been here since yesterday; he lunched and dined with me. On his return to Paris he will tell you what I said. I like, and so do you, this young fellow who has such fine qualities of mind and heart. He will repeat my words to you. You will see how far I am ready, but I intend to go to Paris only in one contingency and for one object, heroic indeed, *Paris summoning the Revolution to the rescue.* In that case I shall come; otherwise I stay here.[1]

Undoubtedly I have confidence in the final result. I have never believed in France more than at the present moment. She will accomplish her mission, the continental republic, and then dissolve in it. From this war can only come the end of all wars, and out of this fearful clash of monarchies can only spring the United States of Europe. You will see them; I shall not. Why? Because I predicted them. I was the first to utter, on the 17th of July, 1851 (amid cries of derision), this phrase: *The United States of Europe.* Therefore I shall be shut out from them. Never did a Moses see the promised land.

[1] Victor Hugo left Brussels for Paris on the 5th of September, just after the Republic had been proclaimed.

At the present moment to be a democrat is to be a patriot; to defend Paris is to defend the world. *Homo sum;* I defend Paris.

Your letter brought tears to my eyes. How you love me and how I love you!   V.

Charles, Claretie, and Frédéric are just starting for Virton. Fighting is going on near there, at Carignan. They are going to see what they can of the battle.

IV. AFTER THE FALL OF THE EMPIRE.
1870–1882.

I.

To GENERAL TROCHU.

PARIS, 25*th September*, 1870.

GENERAL, — An old man is of small account, but example is something. I wish to go where there is danger, and to go unarmed. I am told that a permit signed by you is necessary. I beg you to send it me.

Faithfully yours,

VICTOR HUGO.

II.

To PAUL MEURICE.

BORDEAUX, 18*th February*, 1871.

DEAR MEURICE, — This is my first spare moment, and I devote it to you, to Mme. Meurice, and to Auguste Vacquerie. Ah, how I miss you all! My heart misses you, my conscience misses you, my mind misses you. Never have I felt the want of you so much as just now when you are no longer with me.

I am not sure if this letter will reach you. The vagaries of the Prussians are as difficult to foresee as to set bounds to. Here we are at last. A trying journey. Victor has written and told you about it. We arrived on the 14th at two o'clock; no rooms to be had; all the hotels full. At ten o'clock at night we did not know where we should sleep. At last we have a roof over our heads, and even kindly hosts.

Now, between you and me, the situation is frightful. The Chamber is beyond belief; we are a minority of 50 to 700. It is 1815 added to 1851 (alas! the same figures, with a slight change in their order). They began by refusing to listen to Garibaldi, who took his departure. We think — Louis Blanc, Schoelcher, and I — that we, too, shall come to that at last.

There will probably be nothing to fall back on in face of the crushing majorities in prospect but a wholesale resignation of the Left, supported by reasons. This would rankle in the Assembly, and probably be its death-blow. We have a meeting of the Left every evening. Louis Blanc and I make tremendous efforts to form it into a group. A great deal of unanimity and strict discipline would enable us, perhaps, to make a fight of it. But shall we obtain this unanimity? Not a single paper on our side. We are in the air; no point of support. The *Rappel*, if published here, would be of immense service. One of you ought to come. The situation must be seen to be understood. In Paris you have no idea of it.

How far off are the delightful days spent in your hospitable house! The bombs were bursting over my head, but I was near your heart.

19th February.

I add a few lines in haste. You know that the people of Bordeaux gave me a splendid ovation the day after my arrival. Fifty thousand men on the Grande

Place shouted: *Vive Victor Hugo!* The next day the Assembly lined the square with infantry, cavalry, and artillery. As I had cried, *Vive la République!* and as fifty thousand voices had repeated the cry, the Assembly trembled. It declared itself insulted and threatened. However, I have not raised any objection. I reserve myself for the decisive moment.

This view is shared by the meeting of the Left, which includes Louis Blanc, Schoelcher, Joigneaux, Martin-Bernard, Langlois, Lockroy, Gent, Brisson, etc., and which has elected me its chairman. Yesterday very important questions were discussed: the future Thiers-Bismarck treaty, the unheard-of intolerance of the Assembly, the probability of a wholesale resignation. The Assembly is believed capable of refusing to hear any speaker from the Left on the treaty of peace. Needless to say, I shall do all that is required of me in that matter.

This morning the president of the national club of Bordeaux came to place its rooms at my disposal. The sympathy with me in the town is very great. I am popular in the street and unpopular in the Assembly. Good. And I embrace you.

III.

PREFECT *to* PAUL MEURICE, 18, *Rue de Valois, Paris.*

BORDEAUX, 14*th March*, 1871, 12.55 A. M.

M. Victor Hugo sends you the following telegram: *Terrible calamity. Charles died this evening, the 13th. Apoplectic seizure. Victor must return immediately.*

IV.

To PAUL MEURICE *and* AUGUSTE VACQUERIE.

14th *March*, 1871.

DEAR FRIENDS, — I cannot see, my eyes are full of tears as I write; I can hear Alice's sobs. My heart is shattered. Charles is dead.

Yesterday morning we had breakfasted cheerfully together with Louis Blanc and Victor. I was giving a farewell dinner at eight o'clock that evening to several friends in the Lanta restaurant. Charles took a cab to drive there, giving orders to stop at a café which he mentioned. He was alone in the cab. On reaching the café the driver opened the door of the cab and found Charles dead. He had been seized with a sudden congestion followed by hemorrhage. The poor corpse was brought back to us, and I covered it with kisses.

For some weeks Charles had not been well. The bronchitis which he caught doing duty as artilleryman during the siege of Paris had become worse. We meant to go to Arcachon to set him up. He would have drunk pine water. We were looking forward to spending a week or two together there. All this has come to an end.

Our dear old Charles, so kindly, so gentle, with such a lofty mind and such great ability, is gone. I am overwhelmed.

I sent you a telegram. By the time these few lines reach you, I imagine Victor will be on his way back to Bordeaux. I intend to take Charles with me and lay him with my father in Paris, or with his mother at Villequier.

Love me.

V.

To PAUL MEURICE.

VIANDEN (LUXEMBURG), *Friday,* 19*th June,* 1871.

Your letter! your liberty! We had a flash of delight. All our little circle suddenly beamed with joy in our deep mourning for ourselves and for the fatherland. Oh! yes, come quick. We have so much to talk about. Victor is on an excursion, but will come back for you. We shall all be together again, at Vianden, where every step I take reminds me of you; the exile could think of nothing but the prisoner. What happiness to see you again!

I have been hard at work. It has all increased in a sinister fashion. I think it will make up a volume. *Paris combattant* is now inadequate. The book will be called *L'année terrible*. It will begin with *Turba*, and, after going through the fall of the empire and the story of the two sieges, will end with the present catastrophe, out of which I shall bring a prophecy of light.

Yes, we think it would be well to publish the *Rappel* again at once. Come, my dear and tender counselor. *Veni, spiritus!* Mme. Meurice has behaved admirably; of course she has! My humblest respects to her. How delighted I shall be to see her! All of us here embrace you with effusion. Great mind, large heart, gentle brother and kind master, I love you.

Yes, I did right in protesting, and I stopped the cowardly retreat of the Belgian government at once. It now admits the vanquished ones. This is why I have written of it (in my final letter): *It expelled me, but it obeyed me.* Have you read that letter? How much I have to tell you!

I embrace you over and over again. Come!

VI.

To Monsieur de Ségur, Bishop.

HAUTEVILLE HOUSE, 17*th September*, 1872.

Sir,—I was not aware of your existence.

I am informed to-day that you do exist, and even that you are a bishop.

I believe it.

You have had the goodness to write the following lines about me, which have been communicated to me:—

"Victor Hugo, the great, the austere Victor Hugo, the magnificent poet of the democracy and of the universal republic, is also a poor man afflicted with a yearly income of more than *three hundred thousand francs* [underlined in the text]; some go so far as to say *five hundred thousand* [underlined in the text]. His infamous book *Les Misérables* brought him in five hundred thousand francs at one stroke. People always forget to mention the charity which his large humanitarian heart doubtless compels him to bestow on his dear clients of the working classes. He is said to be as stingy and selfish as he is boastful."

Then follow two pages in the same strain on Ledru-Rollin, who is called "an old Crœsus;" on Rochefort, who was *caught at Meaux with a lot of bank-notes in the lining of his clothes;* on Garibaldi, whom you call "Garibaldi-pacha," *who makes war without fighting,* whose army consisted of *fifteen thousand bandits as brave as mice,* and who *ran away carrying off our millions,* etc., etc.

I shall not waste my time in telling you, sir, that in

the ten lines quoted above there are as many lies as there are words. You know it already. I confine myself to noticing a literary criticism in the passage, the epithet "infamous" applied to *Les Misérables*.

In *Les Misérables* there is a bishop who is good, sincere, humble, brotherly, endowed with wit as well as kindness, and who unites every virtue to his sacred office. I suppose that is why *Les Misérables* is an infamous book. From which it must be inferred that *Les Misérables* would be an admirable book if the bishop were a malignant slanderer, an insulter, a tasteless and vulgar writer, a low scribbler of the basest kind, a circulator of police-court scandal, a croziered and mitred liar.

Would the second bishop be more true to life than the first?

This question concerns you, sir. You are a better judge of bishops than I am.

VII.

To DUKE ALBERT DE BROGLIE.

AUTEUIL, VILLA MONTMORENCY, 8*th August*, 1873.

MY DEAR DUKE AND HONORABLE COLLEAGUE, — It is to the member of the French Academy that I write. A step of the gravest importance is on the point of being taken. One of the most famous writers of the day, M. Henri Rochefort, condemned for a political offense, is, so they say, to be transported to New Caledonia. All who know M. Henri Rochefort can testify that his very delicate constitution will not stand this transportation, and that he will either succumb to the long and trying voyage, or be killed by homesickness.

M. Henri Rochefort is a father of a family, and leaves three children behind him, one a girl of seventeen.

The sentence passed on M. Henri Rochefort affects his liberty only, the mode of carrying it out threatens his life.

Why Nouméa? The Sainte-Marguerite islands would be enough. The sentence does not require Nouméa. By detention on the Sainte-Marguerite islands, the sentence would be executed and not aggravated. Transportation to New Caledonia is an exaggeration of the penalty inflicted on M. Henri Rochefort. The penalty is commuted into a sentence of death. I call your attention to this novel species of commutation.

The day when France hears that the grave has opened to receive this brilliant and courageous man will be a day of mourning for her.

A writer is concerned, and an original and uncommon one. You are a Minister and an Academician; your two duties agree here and assist one another. You would share the responsibility of the catastrophe which is foreseen and foretold; you can and you ought to interfere; you would honor yourself by taking this generous initiative, and, apart from all political opinions and passions, in the name of letters, to which you and I belong, I ask you, my dear colleague, to protect M. Henri Rochefort at this critical moment, and to prevent a departure which would mean his death.

VIII.

To JULES CLARETIE.

BRUSSELS, 31*st August*, [1873].

I thank you for having enabled me to read your fine article on the war, and your patriotic and stirring book. A breath of progress animates your generous mind. A striking drama is that and nothing more; if exalted ideas on man and society are woven into it, it becomes a great work.

You are capable of combating the reaction encouraged by the Empire, and reappearing to-day, in literature as well as in politics, under such *pseudonyms* as *good order, good taste*, etc., *which are lies*. . . .

The words underlined were recently written by me, and have made all the absolutist papers, French, Belgian, and English, grind their teeth with rage, a success which encourages me and will encourage you as well.

Go on. You have a brave heart as well as a charming mind. You have courage and talent; that is to say, the ladder for mounting to the attack, and the sword for forcing your way into the fortress.

IX.

To GEORGE SAND.[1]

1*st January*, [1874].

I am overwhelmed, but not prostrated. Your words stir my heart. You are like an elder sister to me. Those who have suffered know how to console. You prove it, you who are so strong and so gentle.

---

[1] After the death of François-Victor Hugo.

X.

To ALPHONSE KARR.

PARIS, 8*th January*, 1874.

I am touched by the kind words you write to me. Never having wronged you, I could not account for the hostility of which I heard sometimes. It was bound to disappear. There was evidently a misunderstanding. To-day we are friends again. I am glad of it, if such a word can be used in the midst of a grief like mine.

I am now going through one of the most painful ordeals of my life. On this occasion, you advise me to give up politics. Alas! what I ought to give up, and what I am giving up, is everything.

What you style "politics" has always appeared somewhat vague to me. For my part, I have endeavored, to the best of my ability, to bring the moral and the human question into what is called politics. From a moral point of view, I fought against Louis Bonaparte; from a human point of view, I raised my voice on behalf of the oppressed of all countries and of all parties. I think I have done well. My conscience tells me I am right. If the future were to prove me wrong, I should be sorry for the future.

Dear old friend, great sorrows are the meeting-place of kind hearts. My hand presses yours.

XI.

To MLLE. LOUISE BERTIN, *Quai Conti.*

16*th* January, 1874.

MADEMOISELLE, — You were kind to these poor dear things, and they were very fond of you. Now the darkness has fallen. All is gone.[1]

Receive the assurance of my respect.

VICTOR HUGO.

XII.

To GEORGE SAND.

PARIS, 19*th* June, 1875.

You dedicate that beautiful book *Valentine* to me! How can I express my emotion?

As a creator of masterpieces, you are the first among women; you have this unique position, — you are the first woman, from the point of view of art, not only of our time, but of all time; you are the most powerful and the most charming writer that has been vouchsafed to your sex. You are an honor to your sex and to our country. Allow me to bow the knee before you, and to kiss the hand which has written so many exquisite and noble books.

Your books are of the kind which give light and warmth; just now we are threatened with an unaccountable increase of darkness; radiance such as yours is necessary; you set a good example. I love our age and I feel that it has need of light. I thank you for being such a lofty soul.

---

[1] Of Victor Hugo's four children three, Léopoldine, Charles, and François-Victor, were dead, and the fourth, Adèle, had gone out of her mind.

XIII.
To THE COMMITTEE FOR ERECTING A STATUE TO LAMARTINE.

PARIS, 23d *January*, 1876.

France witnessed the appearance of a great poet in 1820, and of a great citizen in 1848.

This poet, this citizen, this great man is Lamartine.

I subscribe to his statue.

XIV.
To THE FREEMASONS OF LYONS.

PARIS, 15th *April*, 1877.

An eloquent appeal has been addressed to me. I reply to it.

My friends among the Freemasons of Lyons are right in counting on me. The philosopher is a fighter, the thinker is a combatant; but the former fights for fraternity, the latter for peace. As for me, the day when I cease to struggle I shall have ceased to live.

Governments, which are all monarchical at the present moment, have brought us, the peoples, into the following predicament, — misery at home and war abroad. On the one side the workman without work, on the other the soldier starting for the battlefield. Hence the problem to be solved, a problem which forces itself on the thinking mind and which contains the whole future of civilization: to make work for the workman, and to take it away from the soldier; in other words, to substitute the work of life for the work of death.

The innumerable questions which rise tragically around us are all, at bottom, the same question. It would seem as if a mysterious need of reciprocal pardon were in the air. One is tempted to exclaim: Let us forgive one another. To forgive is to love. Governments which wage war, and governments which do not pardon, are all guilty of the same crime; want of clemency is a form of war, battles are executions. To make peace is to show mercy to mothers; to show mercy is to make peace among men. Let us not weary, then, of holding high aloft this double standard amid the wrath and the tumult: Republic abroad! amnesty at home!

XV.

To LECONTE DE LISLE.

9th June, 1877.

MY EMINENT AND DEAR COLLEAGUE, — I have voted for you three times, I would have done so ten times.

Continue your noble labors, and publish your lofty works, which are one of the glories of our age.

In the presence of men like you, an Academy, and especially the French Academy, should think of this: that they have no need of it, and that it cannot do without them.

XVI.

To ALFRED TENNYSON.[1]

PARIS, *June,* 1877.

I read your splendid lines with emotion. It is a reflection of glory that you send me. How should I not love England, which produces men like you! the England of Wilberforce, the England of Milton and of Newton! the England of Shakespeare!

---

[1] Tennyson had published a sonnet to Victor Hugo in the *Nineteenth Century.*

France and England are a single nation to me, as truth and liberty are a single light. I believe in the human unity as I believe in the divine unity.

XVII.
To THE MEMBERS OF THE FREE AND UNSECTARIAN CONGRESS OF EDUCATION.

PARIS, 16*th October*, 1879.

MY DEAR FELLOW-CITIZENS, — You offer me your honorary presidentship. I accept it. I shall not be able to attend your meetings, I fear, but I ardently desire the triumph of your ideas, which are mine as well.

The rising generation is the future. You instruct it, so you prepare the future.

This preparation is useful, this instruction is necessary. To create the youth of to-day is to make the man of to-morrow. The man of to-morrow is the universal Republic. The Republic means union, unity, harmony, light, work producing well-being, the suppression of conflicts between man and man and between nation and nation, the end of inhuman exploitation, the abolition of the law of death and the establishment of the law of life.

Citizens, these thoughts are in your minds, and I am but the mouthpiece of them; the time of the terrible and sanguinary necessities of revolution has gone by; for what remains to be done the inflexible law of progress is sufficient. Besides, let us set our minds at rest; everything is on our side in the great battles which remain to be fought, battles the evident necessity of which does not disturb the peace of mind of the thinker; battles in which revolutionary energy will equal monarchical desperation; battles in which force allied with right will overthrow violence allied with usurpation; splendid, glorious, enthusiastic, decisive battles, the issue of which is not doubtful, and which will be the Tolbiacums, the Hastingses, and the Austerlitzes of the democracy.

Citizens, the period for the dissolution of the old world has arrived. The ancient despotisms are condemned by the law of Providence; time, the gravedigger, working away in the dark, casts the earth over them; each day as it falls thrusts them further back into nothingness.

The Republic is the future!

XVIII.
To THE EMPEROR OF AUSTRIA.

12th December, 1882.

I have received, in the course of two days, eleven telegraphic messages from the universities and the academies of Italy. All of them plead for the life of a condemned man.

The Emperor of Austria has a pardon to grant at this moment.

Let him sign this pardon; it will be a great act.

www.ingramcontent.com/pod-product-compliance
Lightning Source LLC
Chambersburg PA
CBHW032222230426
43666CB00033B/733